T0121148

The Old Oligarch

Fourth Edition

LACTOR Sourcebooks in Ancient History

For more than half a century, *LACTOR Sourcebooks in Ancient History* have been providing for the needs of students at schools and universities who are studying ancient history in English translation. Each volume focuses on a particular period or topic and offers a generous and judicious selection of primary texts in new translations. The texts selected include not only extracts from important literary sources but also numerous inscriptions, coin legends and extracts from legal and other texts, which are not otherwise easy for students to access. Many volumes include annotation as well as a glossary, maps and other relevant illustrations, and sometimes a short Introduction. The volumes are written and reviewed by experienced teachers of ancient history at both schools and universities. The series is now being published in print and digital form by Cambridge University Press, with plans for both new editions and completely new volumes.

Osborne	*The Athenian Empire*
Osborne	*The Old Oligarch*
Cooley	*Cicero's Consulship Campaign*
Grocock	*Inscriptions of Roman Britain*
Osborne	*Athenian Democracy*
Santangelo	*Late Republican Rome, 88-31 BC*
Warmington/Miller	*Inscriptions of the Roman Empire, AD 14-117*
Treggiari	*Cicero's Cilician Letters*
Rathbone/Rathbone	*Literary Sources for Roman Britain*
Sabben-Clare/Warman	*The Culture of Athens*
Stockton	*From the Gracchi to Sulla*
Edmondson	*Dio: the Julio-Claudians*
Brosius	*The Persian Empire from Cyrus II to Artaxerxes I*
Cooley/Wilson	*The Age of Augustus*
Levick	*The High Tide of Empire*
Cooley	*Tiberius to Nero*
Cooley	*The Flavians*
Cooley	*Sparta*

The Old Oligarch

Pseudo-Xenophon's *Constitution of the Athenians*

Fourth Edition

Introduction, translation and commentary by
ROBIN OSBORNE
University of Cambridge

CAMBRIDGE
UNIVERSITY PRESS

Shaftesbury Road, Cambridge CB2 8EA, United Kingdom

One Liberty Plaza, 20th Floor, New York, NY 10006, USA

477 Williamstown Road, Port Melbourne, VIC 3207, Australia

314–321, 3rd Floor, Plot 3, Splendor Forum, Jasola District Centre, New Delhi – 110025, India

103 Penang Road, #05–06/07, Visioncrest Commercial, Singapore 238467

Cambridge University Press is part of Cambridge University Press & Assessment, a department of the University of Cambridge.

We share the University's mission to contribute to society through the pursuit of education, learning and research at the highest international levels of excellence.

www.cambridge.org
Information on this title: www.cambridge.org/9781009383592
DOI: 10.1017/9781009383608

First published 2023

A catalogue record for this publication is available from the British Library.

A Cataloging-in-Publication data record for this book is available from the Library of Congress.

ISBN 978-1-009-38359-2 Paperback

TABLE OF CONTENTS

page

Preface	iv
Introduction	1
Bibliography	16
The terminology used to refer to oligarchs and democrats	18
A note on the translation	18
The Constitution of the Athenians: translation and commentary	19
Index	32

Preface to the Third Edition

In the 13 years since the publication of the Second Edition, Ps-Xenophon's *Constitution of the Athenians* has received unprecedented attention from scholars writing in English, with not one but two editions and commentaries. Vivienne Gray's *Xenophon On Government*, in the *Cambridge Greek and Latin Classics* series (Cambridge, 2007), includes a Greek text and commentary on the *'Respublica Atheniensium'* alongside two works by Xenophon himself, the *Hiero* and the *Constitution of the Spartans*. J. L. Marr and P. J. Rhodes' *The 'Old Oligarch': the* Constitution of the Athenians *attributed to Xenophon* (Oxford, 2008), in the Aris and Phillips Classical Texts series, offers Greek text, translation, and extensive commentary of more than 100 pages. On a similar scale to Marr and Rhodes' edition is the text, German translation and commentary of G. Weber, *Pseudo-Xenophon: Die Verfassung der Athener* (Darmstadt, 2010).

In addition to on-going discussion by historians in the context of studies of classical Athens and of Greek political thought, the text has been the subject of a collection of articles: C. Bearzot, F. Landucci and L. Prandi eds. *L'* Athenaion politeia *revisitata: Il punto su Pseudo-Senofonte* (Milan, 2011).

In revising the second edition, I have made minor changes to correct or improve the translation, and have variously supplemented the introduction and commentary, to reflect my own changing understanding of the text in the light of recent scholarship, and the bibliography, to give a fuller guide to the scholarship. In addition to those thanked in the Preface to the Second Edition, I am grateful to Paul Cartledge, for alerting me to various misprints, to Franco Basso for extensive and on-going discussion of the problems of this fascinating text, and to Melvin Cooley for careful proof-reading.

August 2017

Robin Osborne
King's College Cambridge

INTRODUCTION

This short tract is preserved among the works of Xenophon, under the title *The Constitution of the Athenians*. It was already suggested in antiquity that it was not by Xenophon's hand (see Diogenes Laertius *Lives of the Philosophers* 2.57). It is quite unlike other works of Xenophon in both style and thought. We have, however, no direct evidence for who did write it, or for the date at which it was written.[1] All conclusions have to be derived from the work itself.

The work itself is peculiar. It begins abruptly, and ends with a whimper, with a series of apparent afterthoughts. But the work is also peculiarly interesting. It sets out to explain how the political arrangements at Athens, whatever their faults, are excellently designed to ensure the survival and health of democracy. It does so by describing those political arrangements and their relationship to Athens' situation, both in general terms and with reference to certain particular events. The author identifies himself as an Athenian (1.12, 2.12), and tries to show that it is reasonable for Athenians like himself, who do not approve of Athens' putting power into the hands of the masses rather than the élite, nevertheless to make no active attempt to subvert its democratic constitution.

But if this work would be interesting whatever the date and circumstances in which it was composed, its precise historical significance and importance depend entirely on when and why it was written. That it belongs to the classical period, indeed more or less to the life-time of Xenophon, who lived from c.430 to c.350 BC, has been generally accepted.[2] But within this broad range a wide variety of particular dates have been suggested. Arriving at a date is closely related to establishing the purpose of the work.

Why was *The Constitution of the Athenians* written?

'As to the constitution of the Athenians, I give no praise to their choice of this form of constitution, because this choice entails preferring the interests of bad men to those of good men; this is why I do not praise it. But since this is their decision, I shall demonstrate that they preserve their constitution well...' So begins this tract, as if continuing a conversation. Throughout the work the author addresses himself to objections which might be made, virtually carrying on a dialogue with a sceptical interlocutor (cf. esp. 1.5–6). This is quite different from what we find in other short works surviving among Xenophon's writings. Although use of the first person is common in those works – *The Constitution of the Spartans* begins 'I was amazed when I once realised...', and *Ways and Means* begins 'I have always held the view that...' – none of the certainly authentic works adopts this argumentative stance.

On first acquaintance *The Constitution of the Athenians* rambles around its subject matter in true conversational manner. The general argument that the various apparent defects of Athens' constitution and the Athenian way of life are in fact ways in which

---

1   The author has come to be known as the 'Old Oligarch'. I have resisted referring to the author in this way here since it gives a misleading impression that we know anything at all about the person who wrote *The Constitution of the Athenians*, and imports assumptions about the nature of the work. For comparison of his style and thought with Xenophon's, see Gray (2007) 56–7.

2   The possibility that we are dealing with a very much later 'school exercise' has not been much entertained. This is largely because of the style in which the work is written, which is so individual that it seems unlikely to be a possible school product. The work *Peri Politeias* preserved under the name of Herodes Atticus offers a good example of what a high quality school exercise on late fifth-century politics might look like (U. Albini, *[Erode Attico] ΠΕΡΙ ΠΟΛΙΤΕΙΑΣ: Introduzione, testo critico e commento* (Florence, 1968).

democracy is protected rolls up together points about class relations within Athens, about the relationship of Athens to her allies, and about the peculiar advantages of sea power, in a way which can seem almost random. Sea power and its influence are discussed in 1.2, 1.19–20, 2.2–7, 2.12–14. The ways in which Athens controls her empire are discussed at 1.14–19, 2.1–3, 3.10–11. The number of festivals at Athens is discussed at 2.9, 3.2 and 3.8. The issue of the difference between good advice and good advisers absolutely, and good advice and good advisers for a democratic city, is discussed at 1.6–7 and 2.19 (cf. 3.10).

It is possible, however, to see a clear thread running through the whole work, and it is worth outlining the course of the argument in some detail in order to reveal this.

The first section (1.1) sets out the overall argument, that democracy is not to be praised for preferring the lower classes to the élite, but does serve well its own interests. 1.2 links democracy and rule over the sea: the masses row, therefore the masses appropriately insist on political power. 1.3 points out that the masses are sensible enough to leave offices that require technical know-how to the élite. 1.4–6 elaborate that men of every class pursue their own interests, so that the élite would not pursue democracy. For this reason (1.6–7), allowing poor and ignorant men to speak in the Council and Assembly is vital, and in fact the poor do have some judgement. This does not make Athens the best city conceivable, but it does make for stability and keeps the poor from slavery (1.8–9).

At this point, the first instance of what will be a characteristic shift of argument occurs. Mention of (metaphorical) slavery raises the topic of slaves, and 1.10–12 turn to the behaviour of slaves and metics at Athens, arguing that their peculiar liberty is a product of their economic importance in a state that relies on a navy. But the same argument from the self-interest of the common people also applies to the way in which they restrict the behaviour of the rich (1.13), milking them to fund cultural festivals but opposing the old education the rich used to enjoy.

In a similar shift, mention at the end of 1.13 of the self-interest of the common people displayed in the courts leads into the very different context of use of the courts to control the allies, and from 1.14 to 1.18 the logic and advantages of the way in which the Athenians use law courts to control the Athenians are discussed. This raises the topic of Athenians travelling abroad to administer the empire, and 1.19 to 2.5 discuss the impact on the type of armed forces Athens needs of the fact that it is controlling allies through supremacy at sea.

The suggestion that control of the sea brings military advantages leads to a shift to discuss other advantages which it brings, in terms of supplies and a cosmopolitan experience (2.6–8). Athenians not only consumed imported goods particularly at festivals but also imported festivals of foreign gods, and cosmopolitanism therefore links easily to the discussion to festivals at Athens, and the way in which religious and other facilities, which used to be restricted to the rich, have been made generally available (2.9–10), thus returning to very much the topic of 1.13. Wealth being the topic, 2.11–12 discuss the way in which a power that controls the sea can monopolise wealth. This is demonstrated by the example of acquiring the materials to build ships, and so we return in 2.13–14 to the power that a navy gives, and then move (2.14–16) to discussion of the additional advantages that would accrue were Athens an island.

Discussion of islands leads naturally into issues of foreign relations, and 2.17 starts from the notion of alliances. But the discussion of 2.17 moves entirely away from Athens' relations with other cities and back to issues purely to do with the democratic constitution (as in 1.2–9). 2.17–18 deal with collective and individual responsibility within a democracy and 2.19 and 3.1, alluding back to 1.1, sum up the fundamental features of democratic self-interest, insisting once more on the class element.

Although discussion of Athens as a sea power earlier in the work had looked at practice as well as theory, discussion of democracy takes a sharp turn from theory to practice at 3.1. 3.1–9 are devoted to explaining why democracy is inefficient in transacting business, and why nothing substantial can be done about it. 3.10–11 are very difficult to link to 3.1–9. They turn back to Athens and her allies and explain why the Athenians tend to support the 'worse' rather than the 'better' elements in allied cities. The question of factions in other cities seems to raise the question of why there is no open factionalism in Athens, and, without explicitly raising this question, 3.12–13 explain that there are not enough individuals with a sufficient grudge because they have lost civic rights to form a nucleus of resistance at Athens.

Although there are some rather bumpy moments of transition, the way in which a topic raised obliquely in one argument becomes the central subject of the next makes the whole work flow very easily, and very like a conversation (compare below p.10). It might be a recipe for extremely partial coverage, but in fact the author manages to tackle most of the big questions of theory and practice and to offer an analysis which makes sense in political, social, and, perhaps most remarkably, economic terms. This is no mean achievement.

So should we take *The Constitution of the Athenians* to have the peculiar form it does because it has a different sort of origin from other short works surviving from the classical period? Is it, in other words, uniquely close to being a transcript of a live oral performance? Or is the form simply a useful and effective way of getting through the rather wide-ranging series of points that the author wants to make? Should we posit a close relationship between this work and some occasion on which the arguments were aired orally, or should we think that the work deliberately manufactures a pretence that it had derived from an oral performance?

Closely related to these questions is the question of whether the work is to be taken at face value. Is this a serious work, or is it a spoof?[3] Should we take it, for instance, to be an attempt to persuade those who do not approve of Athenian democracy, and who think that the Athenian élite ought to be overturning it, that it is not practical to try to overthrow democracy? Or should we, at the other extreme, take this to be an imaginative composition in which the complacent view of Athenians in the late fifth century that their democracy and their imperial power were unassailable is shown up by putting words into the mouth of a member of the Athenian élite. Are we hearing such a man addressing the rich men of other cities in the Athenian empire and defending himself, and Athenians like him, for not acting against democracy in support of allies who revolt? The spoof funeral oration retailed in Plato's *Menexenos* by Socrates, who claims to have heard it from Pericles' mistress Aspasia, shows that some anti-democratic critics of Athenian democracy had fun imitating the clichés used by Athenian politicians who extolled the virtues of democracy. The frame of the *Menexenos*, and the transparent anachronism of some of its claims, mark it out as a spoof. *The Constitution of Athens* has no explicit frame, and no obvious anachronisms.

---

3 The view that *The Constitution of the Athenians* is a fourth-century 'work of imaginative fiction which perhaps belongs to the genre of literature associated with the *symposion*' has been championed by Hornblower (2000; quotation from p.363) and is also followed by Katsaros (2001).

Distinguishing whether it is a serious work or a spoof depends on our assessment of three things: the internal evidence for its date of composition; its relationship to other literary works, and in particular to Thucydides; and the credibility of its claims.

The internal evidence for date of composition

In the course of the work some historical events are alluded to explicitly, others implicitly, and there are many further statements which might relate to known incidents but which could have been made independently of any particular event. Equally, some events are not mentioned which would, or might, have provided powerful illustrations of the claims made in the text, and the failure to mention them might be best explained by their not yet having occurred.

The earliest date which has been championed in recent scholarship relies very largely on one particular failure to mention a major event. When, in 3.11, examples are given of cases in which the Athenians backed the élite ('the best men'), only to have events turn out badly for them, the revolts of Miletos and Boiotia are mentioned. In Bowersock's view (1966) the failure to add Samos to this list indicates a date prior to 440/39 for the work. However, the revolt of Samos was certainly not a straightforward consequence of backing the élite (Thucydides 1.115.2–5), and the omission of Samos from the examples seems unproblematic.

The date which has been most popular in recent scholarship is the 420s (Forrest 1970, de Ste. Croix 1972, Marr and Rhodes 2008). 3.2 (cf. 2.1) requires that there is a war going on, and 2.16 treats devastation of Attica as a matter of fact. On the other hand, the relatively casual treatment of the possibility of invasion at 2.14–16, surprising in any case, seems incompatible with the permanent presence of the enemy, as experienced during the Dekeleian War from 413–404. Within the period of the Archidamian War (431–21), both what is mentioned and what is ignored have been used to isolate a date in 424. The suggestion at 3.5 that tribute was 'generally' assessed every four years seems to require there having been some irregularity to the assessment. Although such irregularity has been suspected by scholars for 443/2 and 428/7, it is certain only for 425/4. The suggestion at 2.5 that long overland marches are impossible seems unlikely to have been written in the immediate aftermath of Brasidas' march to Thrace (summer 424, Thucydides 4.78). However it might similarly be argued that the rather theoretical language of the observation that all land powers are liable to attack from the sea at 2.13 is unlikely to have been written in the immediate aftermath of the Athenian capture of Pylos and Sphacteria in summer 425, although some have precisely seen an allusion to Pylos in that observation.

Gomme (1962) long ago suggested a date of 420 to 415, and Mattingly (1997) argued that the work can be dated to precisely 414. He bases this on the mention at 3.4 of the festival of the Hephaistia, a festival the arrangements for which at Athens are attested by an inscription of the year 421/0 (*Inscriptiones Graecae* i³ 82), and on the allusion at 3.5 to unaccustomed acts of insolence or sacrilege, which he links to the affairs of the mutilation of the Herms and the profanation of the Mysteries in 415. Together these establish a date after 415, but the discussion of tribute as on-going (1.15, 2.1, 3.5) must date before its (temporary) replacement with a harbour tax in 413. The argument about tribute here seems strong, but the interpretation of *Inscriptiones Graecae* i³ 82 is much less certain. The conventional scholarly view is that the inscription, which is not completely preserved, marks the reorganisation, rather than the invention, of Hephaistos' festival (Parker 1996: 154), and one scholar has suggested that the inscription may in fact prescribe only what is to happen on one particular occasion (Rosivach 1994: 154).

If we are to take this work at face value, we can be confident that it is a product of the years of the Peloponnesian War, before 413. Choosing a particular date within those years depends on making assumptions about the tone of the text: just how knowing and allusive, on the one hand, or naïve, on the other, should we take this author to be? Is the assumption of democratic stability found throughout the text compatible with the fear in 415, which Thucydides 6.27.3 describes, that the religious scandals were a sign of a plot against democracy? This question of tone becomes even more crucial when considering the relationship between this text and other texts of the late fifth century.

The relationship of *The Constitution of the Athenians* to other texts

At various points the arguments expressed in *The Constitution of the Athenians* are closely parallel to arguments to be found in other texts. In particular there is a close relationship with certain passages of Thucydides.[4]

The greatest density of overlap is with Pericles' speech recommending the rejection of the Spartan ultimatum, at the end of Thucydides Book 1. Pericles, at 1.142, discusses the advantages of Athenian naval experience (compare *The Constitution of the Athenians* 1.19–20). At 1.143.4 Pericles notes that in the face of a land invasion by Sparta the Athenians can ravage the Peloponnese, and he notes (143.5) that, were the Athenians islanders, their position would be impregnable. *The Constitution of the Athenians* mentions ravaging the lands of others from the sea at 2.4, and draws attention to the additional advantage, were Athens an island, at 2.14. Pericles draws attention at 1.143.4 to the Athenians having land on the islands, and Thucydides at 2.14 will describe the Athenians conveying property to the islands in the face of Spartan invasion; *The Constitution of the Athenians* mentions the Athenians depositing their property on the islands in 2.16. Athenian inferiority in infantry is noted by Pericles at 1.143.5, and by *The Constitution of the Athenians* at 2.1.

There is also some overlap with Pericles' Funeral Speech, as recorded by Thucydides in Book 2. There, at 2.38.1, Pericles mentions the way in which the Athenians celebrate festivals all the year through; at *The Constitution of the Athenians* 2.9 the enjoyment of sacrifices and festivals by the common people is picked out, and at 3.2 it is stated that Athens has more of them than other cities. And just as Pericles at 2.38.2 comments on the size of Athens drawing all good things to it, so *The Constitution of the Athenians* 2.11 draws attention to Athens' command of the sea meaning that it can dominate the supply of anything (a point made by the Corinthians in Thucydides 1.120.2).

Other sentiments variously expressed in the first three books of Thucydides are also paralleled. The Mytilenaians' observation that they had maintained their independence by flattery of the Athenians (3.11.7) is comparable to *The Constitution of the Athenians'* observation at 1.18 that the allies are compelled to fawn upon the Athenians in order to secure fair treatment in Athenian courts. (That the allies have to come to Athens for judicial proceedings is something noted by 'the Athenians' in Thucydides 1.77.1 as well as in *The Constitution of the Athenians* 1.16). There is some parallel too between

---

4   See de Romilly (1962). The relationship of *The Constitution of the Athenians* to Thucydides is the major reason why Hornblower (2000) regards the work as of fourth-century date.

the point in Diodotos' speech in the Mytilenaian debate, at which he observes that, when it comes to issues of being ruled or being free, men do not calculate the risks rationally (3.45.6) and the observation in *The Constitution of the Athenians* (1.8) that the Athenians tolerate lawlessness in the interests of maintaining freedom.

How much significance should we attach to these parallels? Given that the majority of parallels occur with speeches in Thucydides, four positions are possible. One is that *The Constitution of the Athenians* expresses similar sentiments simply because it was written by an individual who was Thucydides' contemporary and was involved in similar sorts of discussion. A second is that the speeches ascribed by Thucydides to Pericles and Diodotos do in fact closely reproduce what those men said in public, and that *The Constitution of the Athenians* was also influenced by those speeches. A third possibility is that Thucydides, in putting together the speeches, was himself influenced by *The Constitution of the Athenians*. A fourth is that *The Constitution of the Athenians* quarried Thucydides. The first three cases would leave the *The Constitution of the Athenians* as a fifth-century work, but the fourth possibility would make it almost certain that it was not composed before the fourth century (the date of publication of Thucydides' work is not known but is certainly later than 404, although parts of the work may have been circulated earlier). If *The Constitution of the Athenians* quarries Thucydides, it might do so simply for information, as part of an attempt to write a work that could pass itself off as written between 431 and 413, or it might do so to draw attention to the hollowness of the claims and beliefs which it cites.

Can we establish which of these positions is most plausible? One factor here is the degree to which other contemporary texts also say similar things. We might note, for instance, that the description of all the good things that flow into Athens seems to have been something of a cliché: we meet it in a passage from the comic poet Hermippos (frg. 63 K–A), quoted by Athenaios (*Deipnosophistai* 1. 27e–28a) along with similar passages. The Hermippos passage comes from his play *Phormophoroi*, which was performed shortly before 424. The Athenians' propensity for festivals at all times of the year is remarked upon by the chorus of clouds in Aristophanes' play (*Clouds* 298–313; original version 423, revised subsequently). The observation that the allies have to flatter (or bribe) Athenians is one common to Aristophanes: we might compare the passage in the *parabasis* of *Acharnians* (ll. 633–45; performed 425) where Aristophanes claims credit for having held up before the Athenians a mirror in which they could see themselves being flattered and tricked.

Passages which make parallel observations about matters of fact (the Athenians taking property to the islands (2.16), or Athenian allies coming to Athens for judicial proceedings (1.16–18) can hardly bear much weight in an argument for the dependence of one text upon another. It must be true of other matters also, as Gomme comments on Thucydides 1.143.5 of the question of Athens (not) being an island, that 'the idea must often have been discussed at Athens' (*A Historical Commentary on Thucydides* vol. 1, p.461).

Even if we conclude that the case for interdependence between Thucydides and *The Constitution of the Athenians* has not been made, and so resist the third and fourth possibilities aired above, the density of the common allusions should nevertheless not be ignored. It is striking that, although it is possible to find Isokrates thinking about similar issues in the fourth century, the parallels for the matters discussed in *The Constitution of Athens* come primarily from works written in, or concerning, the 420s.

How credible are the claims which *The Constitution of the Athenians* makes?
Before concluding that *The Constitution of the Athenians* is what it seems, a genuine attempt by a member of the Athenian élite to enlighten non-Athenians as to the self-preserving features of Athenian democracy, it is important to look a bit more closely at its claims. In asking whether the claims made in *The Constitution of the Athenians* are credible, there are two separate types of credibility involved. We need to distinguish between the question of whether the facts relayed are credible (e.g., whether there were 400 trierarchs each year), and the question of whether the arguments which the author constructs are arguments which he expects readers generally to find persuasive, even if they are strictly not quite accurate. When, for instance, the suggestion is made that 'those who rule a land empire cannot travel many days' journey from home', are we to expect that most readers would take the truth of this for granted, or that most would see this as a statement only credible if you were as complacent as were fifth-century Athenian democrats? Are these arguments whose hollowness is so patent that we must assume that any reader would have no choice but to take the work to be poking fun at those who make claims of this sort? What we decide about the latter type of statement will depend in part on what we make of the former type of statement: that Plato has the Socratic Funeral Oration in *Menexenos* claim that the Athenians won the Peloponnesian War is one reason for taking the sentiments expressed in that oration as a whole to be being 'sent up' (*Menexenos* 243d).

Much of the data in *The Constitution of the Athenians* is unproblematic. That any citizen had the right to speak in the Assembly and serve on the Council (1.2, 1.6), that violence against slaves could be prosecuted (1.10), that metics were important in Athenian workshops and served in the Athenian fleet (1.12), that the Athenians obliged their allies to bring (certain classes of) prosecutions to be heard in Athens (1.16), that Athenians and their slaves served together as rowers (1.19), that tribute was generally reviewed at four-yearly intervals (3.5), all these claims can be supported from independent evidence.

Even if what is made of the data is tendentious, the data themselves seem sound. We may be sceptical about the motivation attributed to the lower classes, but it is true that generals and cavalry commanders do seem to have come more or less exclusively from the well-born (1.3). Whether the majority of juries voted for the verdict that they regarded as in their best interests rather than the verdict they regarded as just (1.13) cannot have been known to the author, any more than it is to us, but the potential opposition between the just and the expedient is a prevailing theme in Thucydides and in Plato (above all in *Republic*; and see further below p.13). It is a surprise when, at 1.17, we read that there was a tax of 1% levied at the Peiraieus, since by 400 a 2% tax was being levied there (Andokides 1.133–4); but Bdelycleon's mention in Aristophanes *Wasps* 658–9 of harbour taxes among the 'many 1% taxes' encourages confidence that the rate of taxation may have doubled at some point in the last two decades of the fifth century. That one can find in Athens foods and other objects from all over the Mediterranean is a commonplace (cf. above p.6); the idea that the Attic dialect is particularly receptive to imported words seems to be an original one (2.8), but true. The claim that the Athenians will not allow their competitors to sell their produce elsewhere goes against a much-repeated modern view that ancient cities did not interfere in trade except to secure food and military supplies, but it fits with the Corinthians' claim at Thucydides 1.120.2 that the Athenians are in a position to make trade in foodstuffs more difficult, with Thucydides' claim at 3.86.4 that the Athenians wanted to prevent import of Sicilian grain to the Peloponnese, and with the control of goods passing from the Black Sea into the Aegean by means of the Athenian officials at Byzantium known as 'Hellespont guards' (*Hellespontophylakes*), who are attested in inscriptional evidence (LACTOR 1 ed. 4 no.s 121–2). The claim that there were 400 trierarchs each year (3.4) contrasts with the figure of 300 triremes given by Thucydides for the start of the war (Thuc. 2.13.8, cf. Aristophanes *Acharnians* 545), but Andokides 3.8 gives a figure of 400 triremes for the number Athens had in the period after the Peace of Nikias (admittedly in a list of rather optimistic estimates), and in the fourth century Athens certainly had over 400 trireme hulls at times (even if not all were fitted out for sailing). The use of the term *dokimasia* (examination) of orphans in 3.4 is surprising, but that there was a state concern for orphans is well attested (Thuc. 2.46.1). Athenian support for the 'best people' in Miletos (3.11) is not otherwise attested, but it is certainly compatible with the epigraphic evidence, and the truth of the other claims in that section, that the Athenians supported the élite in Boiotia and supported the Spartans against the Messenians (in 462), encourages belief.

Against this long list of what is known to be accurate or can plausibly be reckoned to be, there is very little that is even probably false.[5] The claim that the Athenians 'do not allow' the common people (*demos*) to be the object of comic abuse (2.18) has been much discussed. Scholiasts on Aristophanes allege that on two occasions, at least, specific legislation against comic ridicule was passed. Whatever the truth of these claims, and they have been much debated, the passage in *The Constitution of the Athenians* does not require that there was legislation (a weaker sense of 'allow' is sufficient), and it would not be falsified even if it could be proved that there never was any legislation on the topic.[6] On the other hand, it is hard to think that it would occur to the author to observe that the common people do not allow themselves to be abused unless there had been some incident which had made the issue topical.

The accuracy of the data goes with tendentious presentation. This is an argumentative work, and the data are embedded in an argument. The idea that, were striking slaves not illegal, Athenians would often strike free men (1.10) after mistaking them for slaves because of their similar clothing, is bizarre if taken literally, but it is effective partly because amusingly overstated. We know enough about the rather low rate of tribute paid by most allies to be sure that the claim that the Athenians' attempt to leave the allies with only just enough to live off (1.15) is a gross exaggeration.[7] It can hardly be the case that court fees entirely funded the pay for juries (1.16) or, in the same passage, that the allies were entirely administered by the Athenians sitting at home. It is plausible neither that, but for being forced to come to the Athenian courts, the allies would honour only those Athenians who visited them (1.18), nor that only trierarchs, generals and ambassadors visited the allies. The Athenians certainly did build public facilities for athletics etc., but the suggestions that these were large in number and exclusive to the masses (2.10), excluding the élite, are untenable. Thucydides' and Aristophanes' pictures of the effect of Spartan invasions upon the

---

5   Gomme (1962) claimed that 3.2–8 displayed a complete confusion over the function of Council and courts and between judgement and adjudication (*diadikasia*). But *diadikasia* was the name given to a variety of contested claims and was used in a wide range of contexts in public and private life, and we do not know enough of fifth-century Athenian practice to convict the author of *The Constitution of the Athenians* on this point. See briefly Todd (1993) 119–21.
6   Halliwell (1991), Mastromarco (1994), and Medda in Bearzot et al. (2011) 143–68 for further discussion.
7   See LACTOR 1 ed. 4 pp. 86–92.

Athenians are undoubtedly themselves to some degree misleading, as Hanson (1983) has shown, but the idea that the Athenian masses lived through devastation of the countryside without any anxiety (2.14) must err in the other direction. Far from the Athenians being peculiarly ready to repudiate agreements (2.17), surviving historical narratives suggest that they were quite as reluctant as other Greek states to do so. However litigious the Athenians were, the author cannot have known for certain that they had to judge more court cases than all the rest of the Greeks put together (3.2).

There is nothing peculiar to *The Constitution of the Athenians* in this combination of historical reliability of fact and tendentious presentation of the significance or general truth of those facts. We certainly find the same in Aristophanes, in Plato (even where the facts themselves are reliable), and in the orators. Historians are not exempt from such practices: in different ways Herodotos, Thucydides and Xenophon have all been accused, with greater or less force, of presenting what happened in tendentious ways. The slant of the tendentious interpretation is consistent in *The Constitution of the Athenians* but the degree of exaggeration and misrepresentation is relatively mild.

The crucial question for the historian is not whether some particular facts are wrong, or whether some claims are exaggerated, but rather whether what we are offered is a sociological description that is at all plausible, or might have been considered plausible at the time the work was written. *The Constitution of the Athenians* presents Athenian society as split between two groups, essentially the poor and the rich, each of which single-mindedly pursues its own material interests. The belief that whichever 'class' acquired power would rule to its own advantage is widely shared across Greek political thought, both in the fifth century (cf. Euripides' *Suppliant Women* 238–45 and Pericles at Thucydides 2.37.1) and in the fourth, when it is found in Plato and Aristotle. But whereas Aristotle acknowledges that within states that are democracies because the poor are in a majority, the ruling majority will contain a range of different interest groups, so that it is large states that are the most stable since they have the largest number of people in the middle (*Politics* 1280a), *The Constitution of the Athenians* thinks in terms of two monolithic blocks (see further below pp. 12–14).

Scholars have had no trouble showing that it cannot in fact have been the case that the poor (particularly not the purely urban poor or those with no land) were in a majority at Athens.[8] More important, however, than the question of how carefully *The Constituiton of the Athenians* delineates the nature of the majority is the question of the coherence of that majority. It is massively implausible that the majority at Athens constitutes a monolithic block. Even poor Athenians had diverse economic interests and belonged to diverse communities. Athenian citizens divided between an unknown number of phratries (descent groups) and between 139 demes, where deme membership was determined by the place of residence of one's ancestor in the male line at the time of Kleisthenes. Demes varied not only in size, by a factor of at least 20, but also in situation – some were wards of the town of Athens, others were country villages; some were in the heart of the mining district, others agricultural villages; some were coastal ports, others remote mountain hamlets. The distinctive character of individual demes was picked up both by Thucydides (2.20–21 on the deme of Acharnai) and by comic writers who named various plays after individual demes.[9] By attempting to combine an analytical model with a sociological description, *The Constitution of the Athenians* ends up giving a misleading picture of Athenian society.

---

8   See Marr and Rhodes (2008) 21–2.
9   On the demes see Osborne (1985), Whitehead (1986), and Osborne (2010) chs. 3 and 8.

But if the model in *The Constituiton of the Athenians*, like all models, involves oversimplification, that oversimplification is useful in allowing some of the basic dynamics structuring society to emerge. What is more, the author is honest enough to reveal some of the problems with the model, and in particular that in material terms (1.18, 2.11–12), and even in terms of individual political power as far as the holding of 'risky' positions such as that of general were concerned (1.3), the interests of the wealthy were well served by Athenian democracy. It is very unlikely that this author was the only Athenian whose understanding of the society in which he lived was distorted by ideology, and understanding such ideological distortions is essential to understanding Athenian politics as it unfolds during the Peloponnesian War.

Date and purpose of *The Constitution of the Athenians*: some tentative conclusions
The discussion so far has suggested that *The Constitution of the Athenians* is a work well-informed about late fifth-century Athenian politics, although very willing to offer a distorted view. It is a work which has much in common with Thucydides, but relatively little of the information which it gives can have been derived from Thucydides, or indeed from any other extant text. The work presents itself as a product of the years 431–413 and nothing that it refers to, or might refer to, requires a date later than 414. Although there is plenty of mild tendentiousness in the presentation of its data, the work is not so grossly absurd in its claims that a fifth-century audience could not have taken it seriously.

We are only required to adopt a later date for *The Constitution of the Athenians* if we convince ourselves, with Hornblower (2000), that the work could have been written only by someone who knew Thucydides' text. Believing that *The Constitution of the Athenians* was written later than the publication of Thucydides' work requires believing that someone carefully researched late fifth-century Athenian history and carefully constructed a close relationship to, in particular, the speeches of Pericles in Thucydides 1 and 2, in order to make fun, perhaps in the 380s, of self-confidence in democracy among even the anti-democratic members of the fifth-century Athenian élite. Such a send-up would be effective only if those who heard or read it were themselves aware of the arguments used by Pericles and others in Thucydides' *History*. Such a send-up would be much more subtle and demanding than that offered by Plato in *Menexenos*.

The Constitution of the Athenians is not an overtly subtle work. Gomme (1962: 54) wrote of it that 'This work has little or no pretensions to literary merit, either in arrangement or style; it is not a display. But it is meant to be clever; it is an essay maintaining a paradox'. This sort of cleverness is what we associate with the sophistic movement. It seems very much at home in the 420s or 410s, when the central issue of whether or not anti-democratic Athenians should or could attempt revolution was a live one. Anyone opting for a fourth-century date has to think that the unpretentious manner is itself part of the conceit. Alkidamas' short work *On those who write written speeches*, itself written in the first half of the fourth century BC, discusses (esp. chs. 9–20) how oral discourse is marked by use of common words, repetition, lack of polish, and structural dislocation caused by bringing in material that one has forgotten to mention earlier. If Alkidamas could make these observations, then a contemporary could surely employ them to give an essay the appearance of a spoken speech, whether as a persuasive strategy or as part of a parody. But those who are tempted by the thought that *The Constitution of the Athenians* might be a highly sophisticated spoof have to acknowledge that the parodies that do survive – Plato's *Menexenos*, the speech attributed to Lysias in Plato's *Phaidros* – are very much cleverer and more amusing than is *The Constitution of the Athenians*. *The Constitution of the Athenians* seems much too guarded to be composed so far after the events. If the writer of *The Constitution of the Athenians* was so good at spoofing the political arguments of the 420s, why does he not engage in a very much more thorough-going deconstruction of Periclean democratic ideology?

But if this is not a spoof, what exactly is it? The work lies at the very beginning of the composition of works in prose and is best understood alongside sophistic pamphlets, like Gorgias' *Encomium to Helen* and *On not being* or the anonymous treatise known as the *Double Arguments* (*Dissoi Logoi*), texts which explore how arguments work rather than seeking to establish a substantive conclusion.[10] Although the long tradition of trying to read *The Constitution of the Athenians* as a dialogue, which has been particularly prominent in the Italian scholarly tradition, has never managed to divide the text convincingly between speakers, it is surely correct that this is a polyphonic text.[11] That is, this is a text where the author explores the various lines that people take in attacking and defending Athenian democracy.

The very opening statement 'I give no praise to...' (1.1, cf. 3.1), establishes what is going on in this text.[12] For in declaring that he is not praising the constitution of the Athenians, the author implies that he will nevertheless be conceding that it has something going for it. He is not going to be producing praise of the sort found in Athenian funeral orations (as in that by Pericles, Thuc. 2.35–46 with the classic discussion of the genre by Loraux (1986)), but he is also not going to be uncritically damning. Instead he is going to be exploring the sorts of critical things that people say, and then revisiting what they say in an attempt to understand the features that are criticised, and how the Athenian constitution (in the broadest sense) works as a whole. Sometimes the author does this by conjuring up hypothetical critical voices ('But someone might say', 1.6, 1.7, 1.15, 3.3, 3.12); sometimes he puts words into the mouth of some individually characterised interlocutor ('In Sparta my slave would have been afraid of you!', 'Now these are just the materials from which I build my ships', 1.11, 2.11); sometimes he imagines surprise that has to be defused (1.4, 1.11); and sometimes he simply works through a developing analysis. A nice example of the latter is 1.5 where, after noting the contrast between the discipline and accurate knowledge of the 'best' and the ignorance, ill-discipline and depravity of the people (*demos*), he reflects that it is poverty which causes the bad behaviour because they do not get education or the opportunity to learn. Once we have recognised that this is a highly reflective and exploratory text, its historical value massively increases.

What historical use is *The Constitution of the Athenians?*

What precise historical use we can make of *The Constitution of the Athenians* depends upon its date. Simply at the level of factual information, we will be more inclined to

---

10 On the invention of prose see Goldhill (2002). Oddly, Goldhill does not discuss this work.
11 The case for dialogue is best made by Canfora and Corcella (1992) 460–67; Canfora (1982) offers a translation in dialogue form. For 'polyphony' see Prandi in Bearzot et al. 2011 136–7, 140.
12 The opening is regularly mistranslated as 'I do not approve' (Marr & Rhodes 2008, cf. Serra 1979a), 'I do not think well of their doing this' (Bowersock 1968) 'A me non piace' (Canfora 1982). This gets the tone wrong; the author is not angry (*pace* Balot (2006) 95 in an otherwise useful discussion). The view argued for here is owed to Franco Basso and will be further expounded by him in a forthcoming paper.

believe that data given in the work which cannot be directly corroborated from other sources are correct if we think that this is a genuine late fifth-century work.

If this were a fourth-century work, then it would say a great deal about the attitudes of some Greeks (if this is a spoof we cannot necessarily believe that it was written by an Athenian) to fifth-century Athenian democracy and imperialism. The writing of a work like this at the time when Athens was pulling together allies to form a new confederacy would imply a greater awareness of the potential effect of a new empire on Athenian internal politics than is betrayed by any other extant fourth-century text. The guarantees found in the prospectus of the Second Athenian Confederacy (LACTOR 1 ed. 4 no. 246) that Athens would not raise tribute, acquire land in their territories, impose garrisons, etc., have generally been thought to be there because that is what Athens' potential allies wanted. But if *The Constitution of the Athenians* also dates to the 380s it would suggest that those Athenians with reservations about democracy might also want those safeguards.

As a fifth-century work, dating from between 431 and 413, the work has much greater interest and value. It becomes our earliest literary text in Attic prose. It becomes our earliest prose critique of Athenian democracy, and the product of exactly the society for which Aristophanes wrote his own critiques in *Acharnians*, *Knights*, *Wasps* and *Birds*. It becomes evidence for external pressure on the Athenian élite to subvert democracy, and for Athenians thinking actively about what made subversion impractical. It reveals an Athens in which it is possible to criticise democracy in an academic way, without any expectation that democracy can in fact be overthrown. As such it forms an important backdrop to the successful subversion of democracy in the coup of 411 which brought the Four Hundred to power. It is this fifth-century background that I will further explore in what follows, where I discuss the evidence which *The Constitution of the Athenians* provides for the language of politics, and the place of the work in the history of dissent and subversion at Athens.

The language of *The Constitution of the Athenians*

In many ways the language used in *The Constitution of the Athenians* is extremely straightforward. The author employs a relatively limited vocabulary and is quite happy to repeat phrases rather than engaging in variation for the sake of it. Indeed repetition of exactly the same phrase is employed as a strategy of rhetorical emphasis. But the relatively narrow vocabulary does not mean that the author writes vaguely or loosely. At various points it is notable that he employs precisely the technical phraseology of contemporary Athenian inscriptions. So, to give one example, the term for the territories of the empire at 1.19 (*hyperoria*) is precisely the term found in inscriptions relating to the empire. And in the complex world of Athenian slavery, the variations in the terminology used (see note on 1.19–20) imply that a very precise social situation is being described; in the course of the work the author uses no fewer than four terms for 'slave': *doulos*, *andrapodon*, *akolouthos*, and *oiketes*. But the language of slavery in *The Constitution of the Athenians* reveals a further way in which the straightforward language hides some subtlety of thought. The author deliberately exploits the possibility of using the same language both of those who are literally enslaved and of those whose enslavement is not a matter of legal status but of fact, whether they are aware of it or not. This move is used most effectively at 1.11 (see note).

One of the most interesting aspects of *The Constitution of the Athenians* is the language in which it describes the Athenian mass and élite. As well as using *demos* (people) to refer in particular to the common people as well as generally to the whole populace, *The Constitution of the Athenians* repeatedly uses a range of evaluative terms to distinguish the rich and the poor. The élite are sometimes described as 'rich' (*plousioi*) or as the 'few' (*oligoi*), but they are also referred to as the 'best' (*aristoi, beltistoi*), as 'good' (*chrestoi*), and as 'most capable' or 'most powerful' (*dunatotatoi*). The mass are described as 'many' (*polloi*) or as 'poor' (*penetes*), but also as 'worse' (*cheirous*) or 'worst' (*kakistoi*) and as 'bad' (*poneroi* – etymologically those whose lives are characterised by poverty (*penia*) and labour (*ponos*)).

This use of evaluative terms, generally with strong overtones of moral approval or disapproval, goes back a long way in Greek literature. Already, in the encounter between Odysseus and Thersites in the Achaean assembly in *Iliad* 2, Odysseus claims that Thersites is the worst man to have come on the expedition (2.248). In his description of the political situation at Athens, Solon claims to have made laws fair to 'good' (*agathos*) and 'bad' (*kakos*) alike (frg. 36 line 18 West), but not to have given the 'bad' (*kakoi*) equal shares of the fertile earth with the 'good' (*esthloi*) (frg. 34 lines 8–9 West). From the context it is clear that Solon is not here concerned with distinctions of moral worth as such, but with distinctions of social and economic status.

Use of evaluative language to distinguish mass and élite in fifth-century Athens became, however, far less regular. There had been what Adkins (1960 ch. 9) calls 'The infiltration of morality', and first *kakos* ('bad') and subsequently *agathos* ('good') and other similar terms came to refer to success and failure in moral as well as in other matters, rather than to a particular life-style or status. There are some traces of the evaluative usage in Aristophanes, but in contexts where a degree of 'send-up' has been suspected.[13] In Thucydides we find no instance where evaluative terms are straightforwardly used as status terms: what is 'good' in Thucydides and in the mouth of his speakers, is good for some purpose, and even passages which initially seem to employ an evaluative term in a status sense rescue the evaluation by some qualification that they go on to make.[14] Thucydides is, however, peculiarly careful in this. The continuation of Thucydides' history by an unknown hand, which survives only on papyrus fragments and is known as the *Hellenika Oxyrhynchia*, makes use of evaluative terminology of status groups when it tells us that in Athens in 395 the aggressive policy pursued by the Council was opposed by the 'well known' (*gnorimoi*) and 'charming' (*charientes*) (6.2 Bartoletti, 9.2 Chambers), and that 'the respectable' (*epieikeis*) and those who had property (i.e. large amounts of property) were happy with the existing situation' (6.3 Bartoletti, 9.3 Chambers). Xenophon, likewise, in *Hellenika* both puts a status use of 'best' (*beltistos*) into the mouths of some Athenians commenting on Alkibiades' return (1.4.16), and uses the term for the Mantineian upper class (5.2.6). But Xenophon also has Theramenes insist on understanding both 'best' (*beltistos*) and other evaluative terms as evaluative when he objects 'that it seemed strange to him that the best of the citizens who wanted to take part should be numbered at 3,000, as if the fine and good (*kaloi kai agathoi*) necessarily were that many in

---

13 Note especially the use of *poneros* and *chrestos* at the end of the *parabasis* of *Frogs* (727–37) and the effect of its framing by a pointedly disputed use of *gennadas* in 738–40. See Goldhill (1991) 203–4.

14 Compare, for example, Thucydides 6.53.2: 'instead of testing the informers, the Athenians treated everything with suspicion, and on the pledged testimony of *poneroi* men arrested and imprisoned citizens who were very *chrestos*, considering that it was more useful (*chresimoteron*) to sift the affair and discover than, because of the *poneria* of an informer, to let someone get off who had been accused but seemed to be someone *chrestos*'. At 8.48.6 where the *kaloi kagathoi* are mentioned it is explicitly 'those given the name *kaloi kagathoi*'.

number and that there couldn't be men who needed to be taken seriously (*spoudaioi*) outside that number, or bad men (*poneroi*) included in it' (2.3.19).

This evidence suggests that in the late fifth and early fourth century the use of evaluative terms as status terms was becoming more restricted and widely acknowledged as tendentious. It is to be noted that the central terms of positive evaluation, above all *agathos*, seem to have ceased to be possible class or political terms and that even the phrase *kalos kai agathos* was itself being reclaimed from political use. The *Hellenika Oxyrhynchia* puts to political use terms which belong on the edge of evaluative vocabulary – indeed one might dispute whether 'well-known' or 'charming' were evaluative terms at all.

The Constitution of the Athenians fits very much into this pattern. *Agathos* ('good', but translated here as 'excellent' to distinguish it from *chrestos*) is never used in this work as a status term, but always retains its evaluative force. Terms such as *gennaios* are in origin evaluative of birth, rather than terms referring to some other sort of achievement that have been transferred to status. The author seems to attempt in 1.3 to make the case for the *chrestoi* ('good', but etymologically connected to the verb 'to use') really being those who are most 'useful'. His repeated coupling of terms should be read as an attempt to persuade the reader of the identity of the terms (e.g. 'noble and good' 1.2, 'rich and good' 1.4, 1.14). When, at 2.19, he claims that the Athenian people know who are 'good' (*chrestoi*) and who are 'bad' (*poneroi*), he presupposes that the evaluative meaning of the terms maps onto their social meaning. Most of the instances of evaluative terminology in a purely political sense occur near the beginning of the work (with a concentration also in 3.10–11), as if use of those terms is a way of establishing the author's political position and, once that is established, straightforward descriptives ('rich' 1.2, 4, 11, 13, 14; 2.10, 14, 18, 'mob' [*ochlos*] 2.10) can be substituted. We have a unique insight here, if this is a late fifth-century work, into the continual contestation of moral language and the manoeuvring for position that was going on in political debate. Having read this text we can appreciate more sharply what Aristophanes, Thucydides and other writers are doing when they use evaluative language.

The Constitution of the Athenians, dissent and subversion of democracy at Athens

The tensions over political vocabulary relate closely to the development of political theory and its interaction with political practice. This is a second area in which *The Constitution of the Athenians* is a text of great historical importance. I look here at how the analysis which it gives of the strengths and weaknesses of democracy relates to the actual subversion of democracy in 411.[15]

The labelling of groups of men as 'best' or 'good' begs the question 'best at what?', 'good in what?' The overall argument of the work is that although democracy may not be good absolutely, good for the wealthy, or even good for the *polis* (1.6–8), it is nevertheless good for itself (1.1, 3.1). Democracy is the self-interested rule of the poor majority (2.19). If we compare the so-called 'Constitutions debate' in Herodotos 3.80–82, we see that the issue of what is the best government, although initially framed by Otanes in moral terms, is then addressed by the other participants as 'what is the form of government least likely to collapse?' The author of *The Constitution of the Athenians* only occasionally uses the language of expediency (1.13, 2.19, 3.11), but

---

[15] See further, Osborne (2010) ch. 13.

his argument is that the way in which the Athenians arrange their political affairs is expedient for democracy. Expediency is the only criterion here because the question is not about whether the system is fair – it is a basic assumption that it is not – but whether the system has weaknesses which those opposed to it should be able to exploit to bring it down. Effectiveness, not morality, is the issue.

Aristophanes, in *Knights* and in other plays, suggests that popular politicians in the 420s sometimes sought to increase support for themselves by claiming that others were engaged in subversive activity (see note on 2.15). Thucydides' treatment of Alkibiades (5.53, 45; 6.15) indicates that individual charismatic leaders could create significant anxiety among the people that they might use their charm to set themselves up as tyrants. But we have no evidence for any efforts to subvert democracy until after the defeat in 413 of the Athenian expedition to Sicily. When the threat came, it was a consequence of Athenian loss of confidence in democratic procedure. Thucydides says (8.1) that when news of the disaster came to Athens the Athenians were harsh on the politicians who had helped to encourage the expedition 'as if they themselves had not voted for it'. But the Athenian action of establishing a committee of ten *probouloi* ('pre-counsellors') to consider matters before they were discussed by the Council and Assembly suggests that the Athenians recognised that there was a problem with the decision-making framework, not simply with individual unwise advisers. One of the criticisms that *The Constitution of the Athenians* makes of democracy is that individuals are made scapegoats for particular decisions (2.17). We should ask whether the knowledge, or public airing, of such criticism may not itself have helped to secure the appointment of the *probouloi*.

The Constitution of the Athenians suggests that Athenian democracy is protected because the number of those unjustly deprived of civic rights was small. The affair of the mutilation of the Herms and profanation of the Mysteries led to the condemnation and confiscation of the property of a number of distinguished Athenians, of whom Alkibiades is only the best known. Thucydides relates the part played by Alkibiades in bringing about the oligarchic coup (for all that he was later crucial to its downfall), and we simply do not know whether any others of those in exile as a consequence of the affairs of the Herms and Mysteries played any part. But we should note that Thucydides records of Antiphon (8.68.1), one of the leaders of the Four Hundred, that he was held in suspicion by the masses, and the events of 415–4 had no doubt increased fear of exile among those who were conscious that the people were suspicious of them.

The success of the coup of the Four Hundred depended on many factors, including fear of violence (a factor notably absent from the picture painted by *The Constitution of the Athenians*). But among the important factors we should note the raising of expectations of monetary support from Persia, the acceptance that some people were better equipped to exercise power than were others, and perhaps the recognition that the potential collapse of empire required a different organisation. *The Constitution of the Athenians* draws attention to democracy's financial needs, and in particular the need to maintain naval supremacy. With the benefit of even minimal hindsight, it must have become apparent that Athens can never have stood a significant chance of getting Persian support for its navy. It may have been wishful thinking that prevented the Athenians from seeing this at the time; but the Athenians knew only too well that if they could not finance the navy they could not maintain democracy, and this may have caused them to cling at all costs to any hope of getting money, however remote.

In addition to the possibility of Persian support, Thucydides (8.65) also singles out the abolition of pay, except for soldiers, and the restriction of political rights to the 5,000 men most able to serve the city with their money and their bodies. *The Constitution of the Athenians* makes the point at the very beginning that the Athenian masses leave responsible positions to those who are 'good', but themselves seek offices which carry no responsibility but do carry pay (1.2–3). In this passage the principle on which restriction of citizen rights could be argued is taken to be effectively conceded by the Athenians. The very ambiguity of political language, discussed above, is a major contributor to the argument here: 'the common people (*demos*) recognise that they derive greater benefit by not holding these offices themselves but allowing the most capable men (*dunatotatoi*) to hold office' (1.3). The *probouloi* could certainly be represented as 'most capable', but that description would fit others also.

The Constitution of the Athenians was hardly the blueprint for the oligarchic revolution at Athens. But the inelegant style, tendentious colouring, and naïveté of some of the argument must not obscure the insightfulness of much of the discussion. For all that it may seem to ramble, this work provides a remarkably systematic analysis, not of the formal structures of democracy (for that we must wait for the second half of the Aristotelian *Constitution of the Athenians* of the 320s), but of the ways in which democracy supported itself. It also effectively reassures those who favour democracy that they have nothing to fear from those who are critical: there is no significant body men who have been unjustly deprived of their civic rights (3.12–13), and even some of those 'naturally' opposed to democracy have chosen to settle in a democratic city (2.20). Those who masterminded the coup in 411 worked on precisely those areas where recent events had weakened democracy's supports, by comparison with the situation described in *The Constitution of the Athenians*. They exploited for their own advantages the slipperiness of terminology which *The Constitution of the Athenians* itself exploits. Seen as the product of the 420s or 410s *The Constitution of the Athenians* helps us to understand both the path taken by the oligarchs in subverting democracy in 411, and why it was only subsequent to 413 that any such subversion was ever attempted.

Bibliography

Adkins, A.W.H. (1960) *Merit and Responsibility* (Oxford).

Balot, R. (2006) *Greek Political Thought* (Oxford).

Bearzot, C., Landucci, F., and Prandi, L. (eds.) (2011) *L' Athenaion politeia revisitata: Il punto su Pseudo-Senofonte* (Milan).

Bechtle, G. (1996) 'A note on Pseudo-Xenophon, *The Constitution of the Athenians*, 1.11' *Classical Quarterly* 46: 564–6.

Bowersock, G.W. (1966) 'Pseudo-Xenophon', *Harvard Studies in Classical Philology* 71: 33–55.

Bowersock, G.W. (1968) *Constitution of the Athenians*, in Xenophon Vol.7 *Scripta Minora.* Loeb Classical Library (London) 459–507.

Brock, R. and Heath, M. (1995) 'Two passages in Pseudo-Xenophon', *Classical Quarterly* 45: 564–6

Canfora, L. (1980) *Studi sull' Athenaion Politeia pseudosenofontea* (Turin).

Canfora, L. (1982) *La democrazia come violenza* (Palermo).

Canfora, L. and Corcella, A. (1992) 'La letteratura politica e la storiographia' in G. Cambiano, L. Canfora, and D. Lanza (eds.) *Lo Spazio Letterario della Grecia Antica.* Vol 1. *La produzione e la circolazione del testo.* Part 1 *La polis* (Rome) 433–71.

Dover, K.J. (1974) *Greek Popular Morality in the Time of Plato and Aristotle* (Oxford).

Ferrucci, S. (2013) *La Democrazia diseguale: Riflessioni sull' Athenaion Politeia dello pseudo-Senofonte, I 1–9* (Pisa).

Flores, E. (1982) *Il sistema non reformabile. La pseudosenofontea Constituzione degli Ateniesi e l'Atene periclea* (Naples).

Forrest, W.G. (1970) 'The date of the pseudo-Xenophontic *Athenaion Politeia'*, *Klio* 52: 107–116.

Frisch, H. (1942) *The Constitution of the Athenians. A Philological-Historical Analysis of Pseudo-Xenofon's Treatise* De re publica Atheniensium (Copenhagen).
Gigante, M. (1953) *La "Costituzione degli Ateniesi". Studi sullo Pseudo-Senofonte* (Naples).
Gigante, M. and Maddoi, G. (1997) *L'*Athenaion Politeia *della Pseudo-Senofonte* (Naples).
Goldhill, S.D. (1991) *The Poet's Voice: Essays on Poetics and Greek literature* (Cambridge).
Goldhill, S.D. (2002) *The Invention of Prose.* Greece and Rome *New Surveys in the Classics* no. 32 (Oxford).
Gomme, A.W. (1962) 'The Old Oligarch', in *More Essays in Greek History and Literature* (Oxford) 38–69.
Gray, V.J. (2007) *Xenophon On Government* (Cambridge).
Halliwell, S. (1991) 'Comic satire and freedom and speech in classical Athens', *Journal of Hellenic Studies* 111: 48–70.
Hanson, V.D. (1983) *Warfare and Agriculture* (Pisa; reprinted with addenda Berkeley 1998).
Hornblower, S. (2000) 'The Old Oligarch (Pseudo-Xenophon's *Athenaion Politeia*) and Thucydides. A fourth-century date for the Old Oligarch?', in P. Flensted-Jensen et al. (eds) *Polis and Politics. Studies in Ancient Greek History Presented to Mogens Herman Hansen on his Sixtieth Birthday, August 20, 2000* (Copenhagen) 263–84.
Joyal, M.A. (2001) *Xenophon's* Constitution of the Athenians (Bryn Mawr Commentaries) (Bryn Mawr, PA).
Joyal, M.A. (2004) 'The language and style of the Old Oligarch', in R.B. Egan and M.A. Joyal (eds) *Daimonopylai: Essays in Classics and the Classical Tradition Presented to Edmund G. Berry* (Winnipeg) 221–39.
Kalinka, E. (1913) *Die Pseudoxenophontische ΑΘΗΝΑΙΩΝ ΠΟΛΙΤΕΙΑ: Einleitung, Übersetzung, Erklärung* (Leipzig and Berlin).
Katsaros, A.H. (2001) *Literary Perspectives on Ps. Xenophon's* Athenaion Politeia. Ph.D Adelaide.
Lapini, W. (1997) *Commento all'* Athenaion Politeia *dello Pseudo-Senofonte* (Florence).
Leduc, C. (1976) *La constitution d'Athènes attribué à Xénophon* (Paris).
Loraux, N. (1986) *The Invention of Athens*, trans. by A. Sheridan (Cambridge, MA).
Marr, J.L. (1983) 'Notes on the Ps.-Xenophontic *Athenaion Politeia*', *Classica et Mediaevalia* 34: 45–53
Marr, J.L. (1996) 'Making sense of the Old Oligarch', *Hermathena* 160: 37–43.
Marr, J.L. and Rhodes, P.J. (2008) *The 'Old Oligarch': the* Constitution of the Athenians *attributed to Xenophon* (Oxford).
Mastromarco, G. (1994) 'Teatro comico e potere politico nell' Atene del V secolo (Pseudo-Senofonte, *Constituzione degli Ateniese* II.18)', in *Storia, poesia e pensiero nel mondo antico: studi in onore di Marcello Gigante* (Naples) 451–8.
Mattingly, H.B. (1997) 'The date and purpose of the Ps. Xenophon *Constitution of Athens*', *CQ* 47: 352–7.
(ML) Meiggs, R. and Lewis, D.M. (1969) *A Selection of Greek Historical Inscriptions to the End of the Fifth Century B.C.* (Oxford).
Ober, J. (1999) *Political Dissent in Democratic Athens: Intellectual Critics of Popular Rule* (Princeton).
Osborne, R. (1985) *Demos: the Discovery of Attika* (Cambridge).
Osborne, R. (2010) *Athens and Athenian Democracy* (Cambridge).
Osborne, R. (2011) *The History Written on the Classical Greek Body* (Cambridge).
(OR) Osborne, R. and Rhodes, P.J. (2017) *Greek Historical Inscriptions 478–404 BC* (Oxford).
Parker, R. (1996) *Athenian Religion: a History* (Oxford).
Pritchard, D.M. (2015) *Public Spending and Democracy in Classical Athens* (Austin, TX).
Raaflaub, K.A. (1990) 'Contemporary perceptions of democracy in fifth-century Athens', in W.R. Connor et al. *Aspects of Athenian Democracy. Classica et Mediaevalia Dissertationes* 11: 33–70.
(RO) Rhodes, P.J., and Osborne, R. (2003) *Greek Historical Inscriptions 404–323 BC* (Oxford).
Romilly, J. de (1962) 'Le Ps.-Xénophon et Thucydide', *Revue de Philologie* 36: 225–41.
Rosivach, V. (1994) *The System of Public Sacrifice in Fourth-Century Athens* (Atlanta).
Ste. Croix, G.E.M. de (1972) *The Origins of the Peloponnesian War* (London).
Serra, G. (1979a) La Costituzione degli Ateniesi *dello Pseudo-Senofonte: Testa e Traduzione* (Rome).
Serra, G. (1979b) *La forza e il valore. Capitoli sulla* Constituzione degli Ateniesi *dello Pseudo-Senofonte* (Rome).
Sutton, D.F. (1981) *A Concordance to the Anonymous* Constitution of the Athenians (Chicago).
Todd, S.C. (1993) *The Shape of Athenian Law* (Oxford).
Weber, G. (2010) *Pseudo-Xenophon: Die Verfassung der Athener* (Darmstadt).
Will, E. (1978) Un nouvel essai d'interpretation de l'*Athenaion Politeia* pseudo-xénophontique *REG* 91: 77–95.
Whitehead, D. (1982) 'Two notes on the Old Oligarch', *Liverpool Classical Monthly* 7: 119–20.
Whitehead, D. (1986) *The Demes of Attica 508/7-ca. 250 B.C. A Political and Social Study* (Princeton).
Yunis, H. (1996) *Taming Democracy: Models of Political Rhetoric in Classical Athens* (Ithaca N.Y.).

Oligarchs and Democrats

The Constitution of the Athenians uses a number of nouns and adjectives to refer to oligarchs and democrats. I list here both the Greek term (transliterated) and the English term by which I have translated it, giving the first reference for the author's use of the term, by chapter and section.

	Oligarchs			Democrats	
1.1	good men	*chrestoi*	1.1	bad men	*poneroi*
1.2	noble men	*gennaioi*	1.2	poor men	*penetes*
	rich men	*plousioi*		the common people	*demos*
1.3	the most capable men	*dunatotatoi*	1.4	sympathetic to the common people	*demotikos*
				members of the common people	*demotai*
1.5	the best element	*to beltiston*		democracy	*demokratia*
1.6	the cleverest men	*dexiotatoi*		the worse men	*cheirous*
	the best men	*aristoi*	1.9	madmen	*mainomenoi anthropoi*
2.10	the few	*oligoi*	2.10	the mob	*ochlos*
	the fortunate	*eudaimones*			
2.17	cities governed by an oligarchy	*oligarchoumenai poleis*			
2.18	capable	*dunamenos*	2.18	the masses	*plethos*
			2.20	city governed by a democracy	*demokratoumene polis*
3.10	the better people	*beltious*	3.10	the worst elements	*to kakiston*
3.11	the best people	*beltistoi*			

A note on the translation

The translation here is based on that by K.R. Hughes, M.Thorpe and M.A. Thorpe published in the first edition. However in thoroughly revising this translation I have sought to stay even closer to the Greek, and I taken a different view on a number of issues and particular passages. In particular I have sought always to translate evaluative terms in a way that reveals their evaluative nature. *Poneros* is therefore no longer translated as 'the mob', but as 'bad men', '*cheirous*' not as 'the lower classes' but as 'the worse'.

The translation follows E.C. Marchant's Oxford Classical Text, except in as far as I have occasionally punctuated the text differently (e.g. at the end of 1.15) and have made some sense of corrupt passages at 2.17, 3.3 and 3.5 (where I have followed Brock and Heath 1995).

THE CONSTITUTION OF THE ATHENIANS

1.1   As to the constitution of the Athenians, I give no praise to their choice of this form of constitution, because this choice entails preferring the interests of bad men to those of good men; this is why I do not praise it. But since this is their decision, I shall demonstrate that they preserve their constitution well, and manage well even the other things which the rest of the Greeks think are a mistake.

1.2   So, first of all, I will say this, that it seems fair enough that in Athens the poor and the common people should have more power than the noble and rich, because it is the common people who row the ships and so render the city powerful; indeed, the steersmen, boatswains, pursers, look-out men, and shipwrights render the city powerful, far more than the hoplites, the noble and the good. Since this is so, it seems fair that they should all share in the offices of state by the processes of lot and election, and that anyone of the citizens who wishes should have the right to speak.

1.3   Second, all those offices that bring safety to the state as a whole when they are well performed, danger when they are not, in these offices the common people do not require any share. They do not think that they should share in the generalship by having it allotted, nor in the cavalry command. For the common people recognise that they derive greater benefit by not holding these offices themselves but allowing the most capable men to hold office. But all those offices which involve the receipt of money and benefit for one's household, these the common people seek to hold.

1.4   Moreover, one thing that surprises some people is that they regularly distribute more to the bad, to the poor and those sympathetic to common people, than to the good, but even here they can be shown to be preserving the democracy. For, if the poor, the members of the common people, and the worse do well and such people become large in number, they will increase the democracy. But if the rich and good do well, it is the element that is opposed to themselves that those sympathetic to the common people

1.5   make strong. In every land the best element is opposed to democracy. Among the best,

---

1.1 *Democracy may not be good absolutely, but democracy at Athens makes sense and is secure from attack.*

1.1 On the abrupt beginning, see p.1. For the phrase 'I do not praise', see p.11. On the use of evaluative terms, see pp.12–14. The range of words used to indicate oligarchs and democrats is listed on p.18.

1.2–9 *The Athenians use the élite when they require skills, but the common people take paying office and make the final decisions in their own interest.*

1.2 Formally, all offices of state were not open to all citizens, but at least by the later fourth century the Athenians had come largely to disregard the restriction of certain magistracies to particular classes (e.g. the ban on the lowest class, the thetes, serving as archons; see [Aristotle] *Constitution of the Athenians* 7.4, 26.2). 'Anyone who wishes... to speak' echoes the formula used by the herald when inviting Athenians to speak in the Assembly in response to a proposal from the Council: 'Who wishes to speak?'

1.3 Election at Athens was limited to military offices (and, in the fourth century, the major financial offices). Although the emphasis here is on payment for allotted office, military officials were also paid: compare [Aristotle] *Constitution of the Athenians* 27.2, and the labelling of Lamachos as *mistharchides* at Aristophanes *Acharnians* 597–8. Pay for service as a dikast was introduced in the 450s, and we know that the Council was being paid before 411. Assembly pay was introduced only after the restoration of democracy in 403. But in general *misthos* seems to have been the mark of low-grade public employment. See Pritchard (2015) ch. 3. (For issues concerning jury and assembly pay see M.M. Markle, 'Jury Pay and Assembly Pay at Athens', in P.A. Cartledge and F.D. Harvey ed. *Crux. Essays Presented to G.E.M. de Ste Croix* (Exeter and London, 1985) 265–97).

1.4 What does the author mean here by 'do well'? Throughout the work the Athenian citizen body is treated as made up of two stable groups (see above p.9): however well 'the poor' do, there seems no danger that they will ever become 'the rich'. Birth is assumed to be all important; see particularly 2.19.

1.5–7 The objections here go straight to the heart of democratic theory. It is fundamental to Athenian-style democracy that ability to contribute directly to political decision-making is common to all men and not

there is least indiscipline and injustice, and most accurate knowledge of what is good. But among the common people are the greatest ignorance, ill-discipline, and depravity. For poverty tends to lead them into base behaviour, as do lack of education and lack of learning because of lack of money, at least in the case of some people.

1.6   Someone might say that they ought not to allow everybody to make speeches and serve on the Council, but only the cleverest and best. But in this too they are best advised, in allowing even the bad to speak. For if the good spoke and served on the Council, there would be excellent consequences for those like them, but not excellent consequences for those sympathetic with the common people. But now, when anyone who wishes gets up and speaks, some bad man, he discovers what is excellent for

1.7   himself and those like himself. But someone might say 'How could a man like this recognise what is excellent for himself and for the common people?' The Athenians recognise that this man's ignorance and depravity and goodwill profit them more than the good man's ability, wisdom and ill-will.

1.8   Such a way of life could never produce the best city, but this is the way democracy would be best preserved. For the common people want not to be slaves in a city which has good laws, but to be free and in control – and they are not much worried if the laws are bad. For what you consider not having good laws, is in fact what enables the

1.9   common people to be strong and free. But if you are looking for good laws, the first thing you will see is that the cleverest men make laws in their own interest; second, the good will punish the bad and the good will take counsel about the city and will not allow madmen to become members of the Council, nor to make speeches, nor to attend the Assembly. As a result of these excellent decisions, the common people would soon plunge into slavery.

1.10   It is at Athens that slaves and metics lead the most undisciplined life; there, one is not permitted to strike them, and a slave will not stand out of the way for you. I will explain why this is their local custom. If the law permitted a free man to strike a slave or a metic or a freedman, he would often think that the Athenian was a slave and would

---

dependent on birth or wealth (so Pericles in the Funeral Speech, Thucydides 2.37.1, and Athenagoras at Syracuse, Thucydides 6.39.1). That the common people are unintelligent and violent is precisely the objection to democracy voiced by Megabyzos in the 'Constitutions Debate' at Herodotos 3.81. In Plato's *Protagoras* (320c–323a) Protagoras tells a myth in which Zeus gives to all men a sense of shame (*aidos*) and a sense of fairness (*dike*). But if the common possession of these virtues renders all men fit to vote, it is less clear that Protagoras' myth would justify all speaking and giving counsel. The cynical response given here, that giving men who are not 'respectable' the right to speak ensures that decisions profitable to men who are not 'respectable' are taken, presupposes an Assembly split between a 'despicable' majority and a 'respectable' minority. That there was such a split in Athens and that the success of Athenian democracy depended precisely on the 'mass' reining in the 'élite' is the fundamental thesis of Josiah Ober's influential *Mass and Elite in Democratic Athens* (Princeton, 1989).

1.8–9 The singular addressee ('you consider') appears for the first time here, in a context which makes the addressee's oligarchic preferences explicit (cf. 1.10–12). The model of the city with 'good laws' (*eunomia*), that is a good constitution, was Sparta. Herodotos says that Sparta once had the worst laws but changed to having good laws under the reforms of Lykourgos (Herodotos 1.65). The seventh-century Spartan poet Tyrtaios wrote a poem entitled '*Eunomia*', which seems to have included a discussion of the circumstances and substance of Lykourgos' reforms. See further Ferrucci (2013) 95–107.

1.10–12 *Athens allows slaves and metics great freedom because its economy depends on them.*

1.10–11 There is clearly some exaggeration here, but to judge by Athenian painted pottery, where it is often impossible to tell the status of a person, the Athenians were worried about being able to distinguish slaves (see Osborne (2011) ch.5. Although the non-Greek origin of slaves would often be apparent in the slave's appearance, there were plenty of other non-Greeks in Athens, both freed slaves and others. Slaves were covered by the law on *hubris* (aggravated violence), but the law did treat the body of the slave (but not that of the freedman or metic) differently from that of the free man: slaves could be tortured for evidence – indeed their evidence was only valid if given under torture (Todd (1993) 184–94).

have hit him; for, so far as clothing and general appearance are concerned, the common people here are no better than the slaves and metics.

1.11   If someone is surprised at this, that they allow their slaves to live in the lap of luxury, and some of them indeed to live a life of real magnificence, this too is something that they can be seen to do with good reason. For where power is based on the navy, because of the need for money there is no choice but to end up enslaved to slaves, so that we can take a share of their earnings, and to let them go free.

Where there are rich slaves, there is no longer any point in my slave fearing you. In Sparta my slave would have been afraid of you, but if your slave is afraid of me, he is

1.12   quite likely to avoid personal danger by handing over some of his own money. This is why in the matter of freedom of speech we have put slaves on equal terms with free men, and metics with citizens, for the city needs metics because of all its skilled activities and because of the fleet. This is why it is reasonable to give freedom of speech to metics too.

1.13   The common people have undermined those who spend their time in *gymnasia* or who practise music, poetry and drama; they consider that it is not a good thing because they know that they cannot practise these pursuits themselves. In the case of providing financial support for festivals, for athletics in the *gymnasia* and for manning triremes, they know that it is the rich pay for the choruses, while the common people are paid to be in the choruses, the rich pay for athletics and for triremes, while the common people are paid to row in triremes and take part in athletics. The common people think that they deserve to take money for singing and running and dancing and sailing in the ships, so that they get more and the rich become poorer.

And in the lawcourts they put their own self-interest before justice.

1.14   Concerning the allies, and the fact that the Athenians sail out and bring vexatious

---

1.11–12   This is a particularly interesting passage in as far as it draws attention to the way in which the need to pay the fleet had an impact on the whole structure of Athenian society. Since the Athenians need the money which slaves bring in, they have to treat them in such a way as to maximise their earnings. That involves allowing them the freedom to work on their own (reference to 'their earnings' indicates that we are dealing here with slaves who 'live apart' from their owners, working independently but giving a share of their income to their masters), allowing them reasonable hope of eventual freedom, and not being too strict with them. There is an interesting insight here into how to get the most out of slaves. The author is clearly in no doubt either that we are dealing with a market economy or that among the commodities being traded are freedom of behaviour and personal liberty. The formulation that the Athenians are themselves enslaved to their slaves is a striking one, for all that metaphorical use of enslavement is common in fifth-century writings (see below on 1.18). The sense of this corrupt passage is well elucidated by Bechtle (1996). The connection between money and naval power in Thucydides is explored by L. Kallet-Marx, *Money, expense, and naval power in Thucydides' History 1-5.24* (Berkeley, 1993)

1.13–20   *The Athenians control the élite by the financial demands on them and the allies by use of the courts, by taking their assets, and by the naval skill that administering the allies generates.*

1.13   Although the overall sense of this passage is clear – that the Athenian people are happy to milk the rich by imposing liturgies upon them, the reference of the first sentence is far less clear. In what sense have the mass undermined the athletic and musical activities of the rich? The passage needs to be read with 2.10 on the public provision of athletic facilities. Opportunities for some sorts of athletic and musical activity expanded under democracy, with the development of additional competitive festivals; but the 'court culture' that seems to have prevailed under the Peisistratid tyranny, in which individual performers had been fêted, does indeed seem to have faded. Most of the virtuoso performers of whom we hear in the later fifth century are non-Athenians. The final sentence on the courts presumably refers to the sort of self-regarding verdicts that are satirised in Aristophanes *Wasps*. The rôle of expediency in public verdicts is well illustrated by Thucydides' account of the discussion in the Assembly about what to do in the case of those involved in the Mytilene revolt (3.36–49).

1.14   One of the visitors with whom Euelpides and Peisetairos have to deal when they set up the city of Cloudcuckooland in Aristophanes' *Birds* (lines 1410–69) is the vexatious litigant (*sykophantes*), who

charges at will against the good men and hate them – they recognise that the ruler is necessarily hated by the ruled, and that if the rich and good men in the cities become powerful, the rule of the common people of Athens will last only a very short time. This is why they deprive the good men of their citizen rights, take away their money, drive them into exile, and execute them, while increasing the power of the bad. The good men in Athens try to protect the good men in the allied cities, because they recognise that it is a excellent thing for themselves always to protect the best men in these cities.

1.15   Someone might say that this is the basis of Athenian power, if the allies are able to contribute money. But those sympathetic to the common people think it even more of an excellent thing that each individual Athenian should have the allies' money, and that the allies should have just enough to live and work on, while being unable to plot against them.

1.16   The common people of Athens seem ill-advised in compelling the allies to sail to Athens for court cases. But they respond by enumerating all the benefits accruing to the common people of Athens from this practice. First of all, they take enough money in the form of the allies' legal deposits to pay the jurymen each year. Second, sitting at home, without sailing out in ships, they administer the allied cities, protect those who belong to the common people and ruin their opponents in the courts. If each of the allied cities had its own courts, then out of dislike of the Athenians they would ruin those of their number who seemed particularly friendly to the Athenian common people.

1.17   Furthermore, the common people of Athens profit in the following ways from the fact that the allies' court cases are tried in Athens. First, the 1% tax levied at the Peiraieus is greater; second, if anyone has rooms to let, he does better; third, if a man has a yoke of beasts or a slave for hire; fourth, the heralds do better from the allies'
1.18   visits. In addition, if the allies did not come to Athens for justice, they would honour only those Athenians who visited them – the generals, trierarchs, and envoys. As it is,

---

specifically declares himself to be on official business. Allied fear of Athenian accusations against them is further confirmed by Aristophanes *Peace* 639–48 where Hermes describes the Athenians attacking the wealthy and prosperous among the allies. For allies having to refer cases to Athenian courts see below on 1.16. We know little of the ways in which the Athenian élite protected the élite in the cities, but Athens did formally protect those who were its representatives (*proxenoi*), members of the élite with democratic sympathies (see LACTOR 1 ed. 4 no.s 235–7). The idea that rulers are hated by those they rule is commonplace: compare the Athenians in their speech at Sparta, Thucydides 1.76.1; Pericles in his last speech, Thucydides 2.64.5; Euripides *Ion* 596–7. On deprivation of civic rights, see on 3.12–13.

1.15   Treatments of the Athenian empire traditionally place most emphasis on tribute payment. This passage useful reminds us that, even at the time, the benefits accruing to individuals could be reckoned to exceed tribute. Given the context, it seems likely that part of what is at issue here is the rewards given to successful prosecutors in certain legal procedures; but acquisition of land in cleruchies and by other means is no doubt also covered (LACTOR 1 ed. 4 pp.118–20, 122). The principle of sufficiently impoverishing those you rule so that they do not have the resources to resist you is articulated in general terms at Aristotle *Politics* 1313b18–21.

1.16–18   Athenian allies' obligation to bring cases for which the punishment would be execution, exile or loss of civic rights to Athens first appear in the Chalkis decree, probably of the middle 440s (LACTOR 1 ed. 4 no. 78.70–76, ML 52/OR 131). Isokrates 12.63 and 66 also refer to the practice (ibid no. 204). Compare the Athenians' own account of their practice at Thucydides 1.77.1. The importance of Athenian interference for the common people of the allies is stressed by Phrynichos at Thucydides 8.48.6.

1.17–18   On the 1% tax at Peiraieus, see above p. 7. The heralds mentioned are court-room functionaries (see Whitehead (1982)).

1.18   The flattery of the Athenians by allied spokesmen seems to have been a major theme of Aristophanes' early play *Babylonians* (of 426), and is recapitulated at *Acharnians* 630–45. For the allies as slaves, compare Thucydides 1.98.4, where the Naxians are said to become the first allied city to be enslaved by

each one of the allies has been forced to fawn on the common people of Athens, because he recognises that he must come to Athens to have his case tried and that these are the very people who will decide it, for this is the law at Athens. And so he is compelled to make entreaties in the courts and, when anyone enters, to grasp his hand. So by this means the allies are made slaves of the common people of Athens even more.

1.19   Furthermore, because of their overseas possessions and the public offices which take them overseas, the Athenians and their attendants, without noticing, have learned how to row. For inevitably, when a man often travels by sea, he and his servant take an oar

1.20   and learn the names of things concerned with seamanship. Their experience in ships and their practice make them excellent steersmen. For some of them have practised as steersmen in boats, others in merchant ships, while yet others go on from there to a trireme. The majority can row as soon as they get aboard, since they have practised all through their life.

2.1   The hoplite army has the reputation of being least impressive at Athens, and this is true. As far as their enemies go, they realise that they are inferior to them in skill and number, but as compared with their allies, who pay tribute, they are the strongest even on land, and they consider their hoplite force sufficiently strong if they are superior to their allies.

2.2   In addition, they find themselves in the following situation. For those who are subjects on land, men from small cities can be united and fight in one body; but for all those islanders who are subjects at sea, it is impossible to unite their cities into one location. For the sea is in between, and their rulers control the sea. Even if the islanders could secretly assemble on one island, they would inevitably die of starvation.

2.3   As for all the mainland cities ruled by the Athenians, the large ones are ruled by fear

---

the Athenians after Athens has prevented them leaving the Delian League. More generally, compare the description of subjects of the Persian empire as 'slaves' (e.g. Aristagoras to Kleomenes King of Sparta on the Ionians being slaves of Persia who need to be freed, Herodotos 5.49.2–3).

1.19   For Athenians with land abroad, see above on 1.15. On Athenian officials abroad, see LACTOR 1 ed. 4 pp.116–8.

1.19–20   Athenians prided themselves on their naval skill (cf. Thucydides 1.142.5, and, in the historian's own voice, 2.85.2); Pericles notes, at Thucydides 1.142.7, that the Athenians were in a position to prevent the Spartans even practising in ships. That serving abroad helped the Athenians to build up their naval skills is similarly remarked upon by Plutarch *Pericles* 11.4. What is peculiar about this passage, however, is the stress on the way in which relatively wealthy Athenians, who have slaves, find themselves acquiring nautical skills, at least with the steering oar, as they go about the business of running and exploiting the empire (for the stages of learning nautical skills, climaxing in steering, see Aristophanes *Knights* 542–4). The insistence that the Athenians do practise contrasts with the suggestion by Pericles in the Funeral Speech (2.39.4) that Athenian skill was innate and not learned. On the careful choice of different words for 'slave' here see above p.13 and Whitehead (1982). On slaves as rowers see OR 190.

2.1–16   *Athens' naval power and geographical position enable it to force its will on others, to enjoy the products of all parts of the earth and control movement of vital raw materials, and to conduct raids on other territories while not worrying about raids on its own territory.*

2.1   The Athenian belief that their hoplite force was not up to fighting the Peloponnesians, reflected e.g. in Pericles' speech at Thucydides 1.143.5, was reinforced by the Periclean strategy of avoiding hoplite battles (so, in theory, Thucydides 1.144.1, 2.13.2; in practice, 2.22.1), and surfaces at several points in the Archidamian war, above all in the events leading to the defeat at Delion in 424 (Thucydides 4.89–96). Although the Athenians proved unable to take Melos (Thucydides 3.91.1–3), they were never actually defeated by any of their own allies in this period.

2.2   An example of the concentration of forces by bringing cities together is provided by the Chalkidians uniting in Olynthos in the 430s: Thucydides 1.58.2. The history and nature of thalassocracy excite the interest of both Thucydides (1.4, 1.8.2–3, 1.13.6) and Herodotos (3.122).

2.3   Athenian control over imports and exports is alluded to by the Corinthians speaking at Sparta in Thucydides 1.120.2. By the 420s, at latest, the Athenians were exercising control over the destination of all goods entering the Aegean from the Hellespont (LACTOR 1 ed. 4 no.s 121–2, ML 65/OR 150).

and the small ones by necessity; for no city can do without exports and imports. But these will not be accessible for a city unless it is subject to the rulers of the sea.

2.4   Again, a sea power can do what a land power can sometimes do, ravage the lands of those more powerful than itself. For it can sail along until they reach a place where there is no enemy, or only a few, and, if the enemy approach, can embark and sail away. It has fewer difficulties doing this than the power which resists with a land army.

2.5   Again, those who rule over the sea can sail as far as they like from their own country, but those who rule over land cannot travel many days' journey from their own land. For journeys are slow, and it is not possible to carry provisions for a long time if one travels on foot. An army travelling on foot must either pass through friendly territory or fight and conquer; but a naval force can land wherever it is superior and, where it is not, it need not put in but can sail past until it comes to a friendly land or one weaker than itself.

2.6   Again, diseases sent by Zeus against the crops affect land powers severely, but sea powers hardly at all; the whole earth does not suffer disease at the same time, and supplies come in to sea powers from areas that are flourishing.

2.7   If one might mention more trivial matters, because they rule the sea they have discovered different kinds of festival foods by mingling with different people in different places. Whatever is pleasing in Sicily, Italy, Cyprus, Egypt, Lydia, Pontus, the Peloponnese, or anywhere else, all these have been brought together in one place, through rule of the sea.

2.8   Again, they listen to every kind of dialect, and take something from one, something from another. The Greeks in general tend to keep to their own dialect, way of life, and dress, whereas the Athenians mix theirs from all the Greeks and barbarians.

2.9   As to sacrifices, rites, festivals, and sanctuaries, the common people recognise that every poor person individually is unable to sacrifice and feast, to establish rites, or to live in a great and beautiful city, but they have found a means of achieving this end. The city frequently makes many sacrifices publicly, and the common people enjoy the

2.10   feasts and obtain a share in the sacrifices. Some of the rich possess private *gymnasia*, baths, and dressing rooms, but the common people build themselves many palaestras, dressing rooms, and public baths for their own use; and the mob enjoy these more than do the few and the fortunate.

2.4 A good example of the sequence of events envisaged here is provided at Thucydides 2.25.1–3. On ravaging from the sea see further 2.13.

2.5 On the significance of this passage for the date of composition see above p.4. The problems discussed are well illustrated by Brasidas' march to Thrace (Thucydides 4.78–83).

2.6 Xenophon *Ways and Means* 4.9 makes the point that, when the land is unproductive through crop failure or war, what is needed is money. Diseases of plants are discussed by Theophrastos *De Causis Plantarum* 5.8–10.

2.7–8 See above p.6.

2.9 The author returns to the number of feasts at Athens in 3.2 and 3.8. The distribution of meat from festivals is best attested in the Law on the Little Panathenaia of c.335 BC (RO 81); see further Rosivach 1994. For the interpretation of *hiera* here as 'rites' rather than temples, see Brock and Heath (1995)

2.10 See above on 1.13. The *gymnasion* at the Academy had been much improved by Kimon (Plutarch *Kimon* 13.7). Despite the inclusion of *palaistrai* only among the public facilities and *gymnasia* only among the private, we know of numerous private *palaistrai* (cf. Plato *Charmides* 153a, Plutarch *Alkibiades* 3), whereas it seems to have been the open access to the *gymnasia* at the Academy and Lykeion that encouraged Plato and Aristotle to choose those as places at which to teach. Various private baths are referred to in classical texts: cf. Isaios 5.23, 6.33. Public baths are mentioned at Aristophanes *Clouds* 837 and in an anecdote about Phryne attending them (Athenaios *Deipnosophistai* 590f). Plato *Laws* 761c says that the young men must construct *gymnasia* for themselves and hot baths for the elderly.

2.11   They alone are able to take possession of the wealth of the Greeks and of the foreigners. For if a city is rich in timber for shipbuilding, where can it dispose of it, unless it persuades the power that rules the sea? And what if a city is rich in iron, copper, or flax? Where can it dispose of them, unless it persuades the power that rules the sea? Now these are just the materials from which I build my ships; from one place
2.12   I get my timber, from another iron, and from yet others copper, flax and wax. In addition, the Athenians will not allow our competitors to take their produce elsewhere; if they try to, they will be barred from the sea. Thus I, doing nothing, get possession of all these products of the earth through control of the sea. No other city possesses two of these substances: you will not find timber and flax in the same country, for, where a city is rich in flax, you will find that its territory is a treeless plain. You cannot get copper and iron from the same city, nor the other two or three from one city, but you will find one of them here, another there.
2.13   Yet again, all along the coast of the mainland there are headlands jutting out, or islands lying just off shore, or some strait; so the rulers of the sea can anchor at these
2.14   spots and harm those living on the mainland. They have only one weakness: if the Athenians lived on an island and ruled the sea, then they would be able to inflict damage, if they so wished, but suffer nothing, while they controlled the sea: their land would not be ravaged, and no enemy could enter it. But, as it is, the farmers and the rich men of Athens are more inclined to make up to the enemy than are the common people, who are quite well aware that it is not their property that will be burnt and ravaged, and so live without fear and do not make up to them.
2.15   In addition, they would have been freed from another fear, if they lived on an island: never would the city be betrayed by a few men, or the gates opened and the enemy

---

2.11–12   Behind the claim that only Athens can access the wealth of Greek and non-Greek states are two assumptions. The first is that wealth is created in the marketplace. So shipbuilding timber only becomes wealth when it is exchanged. 2.11 essentially makes the point that all wealth creation is in Athenian power because of their control over the sea, but because the raw materials mentioned in 2.11 are those required to build ships, the secondary point is also made that Athens can effectively control the building of ships. The second assumption is that the marketplace is created only by seaborne trade. Even were it true, as is claimed in 2.12, that no state has its own supply of any two of the commodities, the argument still requires that movement of goods over land is impossible. In fact, not all the raw materials mentioned are plausibly highly localised: wax, most obviously, could be widely produced. And although transport by land was more expensive than transport by sea, it was nonetheless possible. With this passage it is instructive to compare Isokrates 4.92 on no city being self-sufficient, and Plato *Laws* 705a–d, on the advantages of having few resources and no good access to the sea. For the timbers suitable for shipbuilding see Theophrastos *Historia Plantarum* 5.7, Plato *Laws* 705c; for Athenian importation of shipbuilding timber see ML 91/OR 188; see also R. Meiggs *Trees and Timber in the Ancient Mediterranean World* (Oxford, 1982) ch.5 'Forests and Fleets'. Cyprus and Euboia were the great copper sources, Egypt, Phoenicia, and the Black Sea the major sources of flax for linen sails.
2.13–14   For the implications of this section for the date of composition see above p.4.
2.13   For Athenian ability to attack anywhere they like, compare Pericles at Thucydides 2.41.4. Some have seen an allusion to Pylos in the mention of 'headlands' here.
2.14   For fantasy thoughts about the advantages that would accrue if Athens were an island, see Pericles at Thucydides 1.143.5 (see above p.5). For the tendency of farmers and wealthy men to want peace and the poor to want war, compare Aristophanes *Ekklesiazousai* 197–8. The claim that the common people are not worried by ravaging is unbelievable and seems to assume that the common people all live in the town; they did not. See above p.9.
2.15   The degree to which cities at war feared betrayal is made very clear in Aineias Taktikos' *Poliorkemata*, written in the fourth century. There is little sign of such fear in Athens itself during the Archidamian War, despite the frequent jokes about conspirators in Aristophanes (e.g. *Knights* 236, 257, 452, 476, 628, 861–3, *Wasps* 345, 417, 463–70, 474, 483, 488, 507, 953), although there had been such suspicions at the time of the battle of Tanagra: see Thucydides 1.107.4, 6; Plutarch *Kimon* 17.4–7. Such fears surfaced again after the herms were mutilated in 415, see Thuc. 6.27.3.

rush in. For if they lived on an island how could this happen? Nor would they fear any revolt against the common people, if they lived on an island. For, as it is, such a revolt would be based on hope that the enemy would invade by land. But if they lived on an island, they would be fearless even on this count.

2.16 Since it has not turned out that they have lived on an island from the beginning, this is what they now do: they deposit their property in the islands, trusting their control of the sea, and turn a blind eye to the devastation of Attica, for they recognise that, if they are swayed by sentiment in this matter, they will be deprived of other and greater advantages.

2.17 Moreover, cities governed by an oligarchy must of necessity abide by their alliances and agreements. If they do not, or if some injustice is committed, then among so few the names of those who made the agreement are well known. But when the common people make any agreement, they can always fix the blame on the individual who proposed the measure or who put it to the vote, and the rest of them can deny responsibility, saying 'I wasn't there, and I don't approve of it', when they find that it was agreed at a full meeting of the common people. If they decide against the policy, they have countless reasons to hand for not doing what they do not want to do. And if a policy which the common people counselled then turns out badly, the common people accuse a few men of acting against their interest and destroying them, while if the policy succeeds they claim the credit for themselves.

2.18 But they do not allow public ridicule or abuse of the common people, because they

---

2.16   It is simply assumed here that the city of Athens itself is adequately protected by walls, and will not be taken by siege. For Athenian use of the islands see Thucydides 2.14 with 7.28.1 and 8.96.2. The suggestion that abandoning the territory was based on a calculus of advantage recurs in Lysias 34.9. The question of whether the Athenians could manage to ignore the devastation was an important topic of debate in the first year of the war: Thucydides 2.18.5, 20.2, 20.4.

2.17–20   *Democracy exploits the possibility of blaming individuals and protects the common people from blame. It is those who are not of the common people but take active part in democracy who are blameworthy.*

2.17   The important general issue here, and in 2.18, is where responsibility lies in a democracy. In monarchical and oligarchical régimes, the suggestion is, individual and corporate responsibility are essentially the same thing. But in democracies it is possible for individual and corporate responsibility to become separate, and for the responsibility to be associated with the proposer of a motion, or the person institutionally responsible for the vote being taken, rather than with the body of the citizens who in fact vote the measure through. That someone who proposes or puts to the vote a matter which the Athenians do not want discussed is liable to punishment is frequently explicitly stated in Athenian decrees in what has come to be called an 'entrenchment clause': see D.M. Lewis 'Entrenchment-clauses in Attic decrees' in his *Selected Papers in Greek and Near Eastern History* (Cambridge, 1997) 136–49. Although the earliest epigraphic entrenchment-clause dates to the 470s or 460s and is in a deme decree (*Inscriptiones Graecae* i³ 245), the formula echoed in this passage is particularly well attested in state decrees from 431 onwards (and cf. Thuc. 2.24.1 with 8.15.1, 8.67.2). The decision of a speaker in the assembly to emphasise individual over collective responsibility is mocked at Aristophanes *Acharnians* 516–7. For Athenians directing particular blame against the proposers of measures that turned out badly compare the reaction against Pericles in the second year of the war (Thucydides 2.60.2–3, 65.1–4), the reaction to the defeat in Sicily (Thucydides 8.1.1), and the aftermath of the Arginousai trial (Xenophon *Hellenika* 1.7.35). 'Deceiving the people' seems to have been a possible charge against an individual (cf. [Aristotle] *Constitution of the Athenians* 43.5), and the scope of the 'prosecution against illegal proposals' (*graphe paranomon*), perhaps introduced around 416, included the unwise as well as the strictly illegal. Aristophanes *Ekklesiazousai* 195–6 suggests that politicians who were conscious that they had proposed something that became unpopular might make themselves scarce. For the argument that one should blame those who proposed decrees which proved damaging, see Lysias 18.2–3. See also above p.15.

2.18   On the question of what legislation, if any, lies behind these claims, see above p.8. Aristophanes defends himself against the charge of attacking the common people in *Acharnians* 630–32. On those who 'meddle in everything' see P. Harding 'In search of a Polypragmatist' in G. Shrimpton and D. McCargar (ed) *Classical Contributions: Studies in Honour of M.F. McGregor* (Locust Valley N.Y., 1981) 41–50.

do not like to hear themselves abused. If anyone wants to ridicule anyone, they encourage him to attack individuals, because they are well aware that those who are ridiculed generally do not come from the common people or from the masses but are rich or noble or capable. A few of the poor and those who sympathise with the common people are ridiculed, but only if they meddle in everything and try to get the better of the common people. As a result, they do not even object when such individuals as these are ridiculed.

2.19   It is my opinion, therefore, that the common people at Athens recognise which citizens are good and which are bad. But, although recognising this, they like those who are friendly and back their interests, even if they are bad, and it is rather the good citizens that they hate. For they do not consider the ability of those to be naturally inclined to their advantage, but to their harm. But the opposite applies in some cases – that those who are in fact of the common people are not sympathetic to the common people by nature.

2.20   I can forgive the common people their democracy; for anyone can be forgiven for looking after their own interests. But anyone who is not one of the common people, and yet chooses to settle in a city governed by a democracy rather than one governed by an oligarchy, must be preparing to do wrong and have decided that a bad man can escape detection far more easily in a democratic than in an oligarchic city.

3.1   Concerning the constitution of the Athenians, I do not praise the way it is organised, but since they have decided that it should be a democracy, it seems to me that they preserve the democracy well using the organisation which I have described.

But still I know that some people blame the Athenians because sometimes a person can spend a year and still not get business settled by the Council or the Assembly. This happens at Athens purely because the mass of business to be settled means that they

3.2   cannot complete everyone's business. Indeed, how could they, when, to start with, they

---

2.19   The vocabulary of evaluation is here used with a primarily moral sense: the good are morally good, and the depravity of the bad does not stand in the way of them being the most successful advisers. On the potential clash between the moral and the expedient see 1.13 and p.14 above. The sense of the final sentence of 2.19 is disputed; Marr and Rhodes maintain that it means exactly the opposite to my translation here: 'there are some men who actually take the side of the people, even though they are not by nature commoners', but this must be wrong. The adjective *demotikos* in this work always refers to having a populist attitude, not having a demotic origin, and when the phrase 'being of the *demos*' occurs both a sentence earlier and two sentences later it certainly refers to birth; see further Lapini (1997) 218–9.

2.20–3.1   These chapters read as a conclusion to the enterprise outlined in 1.1, but they also introduce for the first time the issue of the political choices of individuals. It is often suggested that the phrase I have translated as 'settle in a city governed by democracy' means rather 'have a political life in a democratic city' (Marr and Rhodes; cf. Lapini (1997) 244–5). But this is to over-translate the Greek verb *oikein*, which simply means to 'settle' or 'live' and to miss the force of '*chooses* to settle', which is rightly emphasised by Gray (2007) 205. The author is not thinking of rich Athenians who take part in politics (he has acknowledged their crucial participation in key offices in 1.3); he is thinking rather of rich metics who might settle anywhere but choose to settle in a democratic city. Note that this point does not particularly concern living in Athens, but in any democratic city.

3.1–8   *Democracy is inefficient, but nothing can be done about it without endangering democracy itself.*

3.1   The Athenian Assembly (*demos*, used here in its technical sense) met forty times a year and had a fixed pattern to its agenda, at least in the later fourth century ([Aristotle] *Constitution of the Athenians* 43). Only matters which had already been discussed by the Council could be raised in the Assembly ([Aristotle] *Constitution of the Athenians* 45.4). Some fourth-century honorific decrees grant a place high on the agenda to business that an honorand brings (RO 64.53–9), and on matters the Assembly is keen to keep a particular eye on it may insist that the Council keeps continuous watch (RO 100.242–58).

3.2   For the exceptional frequency of festivals at Athens compare Thucydides 2.38.1, Aristophanes *Clouds* 298–313, and Isokrates 4.43ff. For meetings of the Assembly avoiding festival days see J. Mikalson *The*

have to celebrate more festivals than any other Greek city – and during festivals it is less possible for anyone to transact state business – and on top of that they have to judge more public and private lawsuits and examine more officials than all the rest put together, and the Council has to take many decisions on matters of the war, many on finance, many on legislation, many to do with what is happening at any time in the city, and many to do with the allies, and to receive tribute and administer the dockyards and sanctuaries? Is there anything surprising if, under such a weight of business, they are not able to settle everyone's affairs?

3.3   Some people say, 'If you approach the Council or Assembly with money, you will get things done'. I would agree with them that money does get many things done in Athens, and that still more would be done, if even more people offered money. But I also know well that the city would not be capable of completing all the transactions that everyone wants, even if someone were to give them any amount of gold and silver.

3.4   There must be a judicial inquiry if someone fails to equip his trireme, or builds on public land; in addition to there are disputes to be resolved every year for those who are to finance the chorus at the Dionysia, the Thargelia, the Panathenaia, the Prometheia and the Hephaistia. And four hundred trierarchs are chosen for each year: there are disputes to settle from any of them who want to argue the case. In addition to this there are incoming officials to scrutinise and disputes over them to settle; there are orphans to investigate and prison warders to appoint.

3.5   So much for annual matters; from time to time it is also necessary to give judgement when cases involving generals or any other offence suddenly crop up, such as if

---

Sacred and Civil Calendar of the Athenian Year (Princeton, 1975). The courts did not meet on days when the Assembly met: Demosthenes 24.80. For Athenian litigiousness compare Thucydides 1.77.1, Aristophanes *Knights* 1316–7, *Clouds* 207–8, *Peace* 505, *Birds* 40–41 etc. The distinction between *dikai* and *graphai* does not exactly correspond with our distinctions either between private and public cases or between civil and criminal cases: *dikai* were cases brought by the injured party, *graphai* cases that could be brought by anyone who wanted to. The duties of the Council are summarised in [Aristotle] *Constitution of the Athenians* 43.2 to 50.1. See also P.J. Rhodes *The Athenian Boule* (Oxford, 1972, revised ed.1985). In the fourth century there was a special procedure for making laws, which did not involve the Council, but in the fifth century no procedural distinction was made between making laws and making other decisions of state, with the Council preparing both.

3.3 On bribery at Athens see F.D. Harvey 'Dona Ferentes. Some aspects of bribery in Greek politics', in P.A. Cartledge and F.D. Harvey ed. *Crux. Essays Presented to G.E.M. de Ste Croix* (Exeter and London, 1985) 76–117. Allegations that members of the Council accepted bribes are frequent in comedy (Aristophanes *Georgoi* frg.102 K–A, *Thesmophoriazousai* 936–7; cf. *Knights* 624–86). [Aristotle] *Constitution of the Athenians* 27.5 claims that the first person successfully to bribe a court was Anytos, in an incident to be dated to 410 or 409. Bribing juries in the courts became much more difficult when random distribution of jurors to courts was introduced ([Aristotle] *Constitution of the Athenians* 63–9).

3.4 On 'judicial inquiries' (*diadikasiai*) see above p.8 n.5. Various tasks that have to be done in democracy are listed here, without regard to which agent of the state is responsible. The focus on disputes is notable; we know quite a lot about the procedure whereby a person asked to perform a liturgy (i.e. finance a festival or a trireme) could claim that another person was more wealthy and should perform the liturgy instead, offering to exchange property with the person in question (*antidosis*, see esp. Dem. 42), but we do not know how often the procedure was invoked. For the group of festivals listed here (apart from the Panathenaia), compare *Inscriptiones Graecae* ii² 1138. For the possible chronological significance of the mention of the Hephaistia, see p.4. The expense for the Dionysia was the drama, for the Thargelia the dithyrambs, for the Panathenaia the games and the torch race, and for the Prometheia and Hephaistia the torch race (see Pritchard (2015) ch. 2). On the number of trierarchs see p.8. On state concern for orphans see [Aristotle] *Constitution of the Athenians* 56.6–7, [Demosthenes] 43.75.

3.5 For the question of whether there is a specific reference here to the mutilation of the Herms and profanation of the Mysteries see above p.4. On the frequency with which tribute was reviewed see above p.4. For disputes over levels of tribute payment see LACTOR 1 ed. 4 no.s 186–9. That there were disputes over tribute collection is further implied by the Kleinias and Kleonymos decrees, the latter certainly and the former probably dating to the middle 420s (ibid 190, 136, ML 46, 68/OR 154, 152).

someone commits an unprecedented act of wanton violence or of sacrilege. I pass over many other things; but I have enumerated the most important, except for the calculation of tribute. This is generally done at four-yearly intervals.

3.6   Think about this: am I not right in thinking that all these disputes have to be settled? Anyone who thinks there is something here that does not need settling should speak up.

And yet if we must agree that all these disputes need settling, then inevitably it takes the whole year. Even though they now spend the whole year in the lawcourts, they do
3.7   not manage to stop people doing wrong because of the number of people. Think about this: that someone might concede that there need to be all these court cases but suggest that the task of judging should rest with fewer people. Well, inevitably, unless they have only a few courts, there will be few people in each court; as a result, it will be easier to manipulate a small jury and to bribe them all to give a much less just verdict.

3.8   Furthermore we must remember that the Athenians have to celebrate festivals, during which they cannot hold trials, and that they celebrate twice as many as other cities; but I work on the assumption that they hold the same number as that city which celebrates the fewest.

Now under these circumstances I maintain that the present position at Athens is inevitable, except that they could make small additions or deletions. But the change
3.9   cannot be great without eroding the democracy. It is possible to find many ways of making the constitution better, but it is difficult to find effective ways of making the constitution better while still maintaining the democracy, except, as I have just said, with slight additions and deletions.

3.10   In this policy too the Athenians seem to me not to follow the right counsel, when they side with the worse men in cities split by civil strife. But they do this advisedly. For if they chose the better people, they would not be choosing people sympathetic to their own ideas. For in no city are the best elements well disposed to the common people: it is rather the worst elements in each city who are well-disposed to the common people. Like are well-disposed to like. For this reason, therefore, the Athenians choose

---

3.6 The emphasis on the number of judicial inquiries, which has dominated this discussion of the courts, is here dropped, and emphasis shifts to the rôle of the courts in dealing with offences.

3.7 The admission that small juries are likely to give bad justice, not just for a sectional interest but absolutely, is remarkable in one who professes to disapprove of democracy. It is a mark of the polyphony of this text (see above p.11) that the earlier complaint that Athenian juries voted for what was good for themselves, rather than what was just (1.13), seems here to be forgotten.

3.8 See above on 3.2. Hansen has calculated the number of days on which the courts met as being between 175 and 225 a year (M.H. Hansen *The Athenian Democracy in the Age of Demosthenes* (Oxford, 1991) 186). The explicit granting of a false hypothesis for the sake of argument is striking here.

3.8–9 *One can think of better constitutions, but few changes can be made to the Athenian constitution without threatening democracy.*

3.10–13 *Athenian policy of backing the common people elsewhere has been shown by exceptions to be in its interests. Athens unjustly deprives few enough citizens of civic rights not to be in danger from such people.*

3.10   This picks up on arguments at 1.5–6. It is characteristic that the author first claims that he thinks the Athenians decision to back the 'worse' is wrong and then provides the arguments which show that the policy has a rationale. Rather than amending the text to distance the author from the sentiment by reading: 'Another policy in which the Athenians seem not to be right' (cf.1.16), we should emphasise the moral element in the initial judgement that the Athenians do not act rightly, and the pragmatic element in the explanation of their action. The problem of civil strife within cities much exercised classical Greek writers and political theorists. Thucydides maintains (3.82.1) that the polarisation of the Greek world between Athens and Sparta made civil strife more serious, and he gives an extended analysis of civil strife on Corcyra (3.70–85, with authorial comment at 3.82–3).

3.11 what suits them. Whenever they have tried to side with the best people, it has not been in their interests: in a short time the common people were enslaved in Boiotia; when they sided with the best people in Miletos, in a short time they revolted and massacred the common people; and when they sided with the Spartans, and not the Messenians, in a short time the Spartans had subjugated the Messenians and were at war with the Athenians.

3.12 Someone might suggest that no one has been unjustly deprived of civic rights at Athens. I maintain that there are some who have been deprived of civic rights unjustly, but they are few. But it needs more than a few to attack the democracy at Athens, since the situation is that one must not bear in mind people who have been justly deprived

3.13 of civic rights, but if any have been deprived unjustly. And how could anyone think that the many have been deprived of civic rights at Athens unjustly, since it is the common people who fill the offices? Men lose their rights at Athens through not ruling justly, or not saying or doing what is just. In view of this one cannot believe that there is anything to fear at Athens from those who have been deprived of civic rights.

3.11 The reference to Boiotia must be to the events between the Athenian victory at Oinophyta in 458 or 457 and the Athenian defeat at Koroneia in 447, but exactly what happened in those years is not clear. Aristotle *Politics* 1302b25–30 uses the events in Boiotia after the battle of Oinophyta as an example of a case where democracy was destroyed because the wealthy despised its disorganisation and lack of law. Both the Thebans, in their speech about the fate of the Plataeans, and Pagondas, the Theban Boiotarch, in his speech before the battle of Delion, claim that the Athenians made themselves masters of Boiotia in these years by exploiting civil strife (Thucydides 3.62.5, 4.92.6). For Miletos see LACTOR 1 ed. 4 no.218 with ML43/OR 123, 143. In the case of the Spartans and Messenians the allusion is to Athenian support for Sparta against the helot revolt in 462: Thucydides 1.102. It is worth noting that the helots here are effectively assimilated to the common people in other Greek cities, whereas they would more normally be assimilated to slaves.

3.12–13 Loss of civic rights (*atimia*) in the classical period could be partial or total, temporary or permanent (Todd (1993) 142–3). At one end of the scale a man might temporarily lose his right to hold office or take active part in democracy because he was a public debtor. At the other end of the scale a man might be banned from public life, from certain public places, and from appearing in court, although he would retain private rights and could not be killed or harmed by others. Loss of civic rights did not necessitate going into exile, although many preferred exile to the restricted life that they could otherwise lead. Exiles are important sources of civil strife throughout Greek history. We in fact know of more cases of execution (or suicide, see Plutarch *Nikias* 6, *Aristeides* 26.5 on Paches) by men found guilty of ruling unjustly than of deprivation of civic rights.

3.13 Does this work end with a whimper (above p.1)? Although 3.1 and 3.8 seem twice to attempt to round off the work by reference back to the very opening sentences, the closing sections do play a significant part in the argument. The author moves from essentially theoretical considerations to close consideration of practice, and addresses for the first time the question of the personnel available for any anti-democratic movement. The repetition five times in the last two sections of the phrase 'at Athens' hammers home the point that whatever one might expect in other cities, at Athens there simply is no body of men desperate to overturn the existing constitution. The author's confidence in this constitutes one argument why the work is unlikely to date after the trials and condemnation of those found guilty of mutilating the Herms and profaning the Mysteries.

INDEX

References in *italic* script are to pages and refer to editorial material.
References in the form **1.2**, **2.10**, **3.7** etc. are to chapters and sections.

Alkibiades, *13, 15*

Alkidamas, *10*

Andokides, *8*

Antiphon, *15*

Aristophanes, *6, 7, 8, 9, 12, 13, 14, 15, 19, 21, 22, 23, 25, 26, 27, 28*

Aristotle, *9, 16, 22, 24, 26, 27, 28, 30*

Assembly, *2, 7, 15, 19, 27–8*, **1.6**, **1.9**, **2.17**, **3.1–3**

atimia (loss of civic rights) *3, 15, 16, 22*, **1.14**, **3.12–13**

athletics, *8*, **1.13**, **2.10**

authorship, *1*

baths, **2.10**

Boiotia, *4, 8*, **3.11**

Brasidas, *4, 24*

bribery, *6*, **3.3**, **3.7**

building, public **2.9–10**

citizenship, *9, 15, 16*, **1.2**, **1.6**, **1.12**, **1.14**, **3.12–13**

class struggle, *2, 9, 13–14*

comic drama, regulation of. *8*, **2.18**

Council, *2, 7, 13, 15, 19*, **1.6**, **3.1–6**

credibility of work, *3–4, 7–10*

date of composition, *1–11*

democracy, theory of. *2, 3, 14–15*, **1.5–7**, **2.17**

dokimasia (examination) *8*, **3.4**

education, **1.5**, **1.13**

empire, *2, 5, 6, 8, 12*, **1.14–2.6**, **3.10–11**

Euripides, *Ion 22; Suppliant Women 9*

festivals, *2, 5, 6*, **1.13**, **2.9**, **3.2**, **3.4**, **3.8**

Four Hundred, *12, 15–16*

freedom of speech, **1.12**, **2.18**

funeral oration *3, 5, 7, 11*

generals, *7, 8, 10*, **1.3**, **2.18**, **3.5**

Hellenika Oxyrhynchia 13–14

Hellespontophylakes, *8*

Hephaistia, *4–5*, **3.4**

Hermippos, comic poet, *6*

Herms, mutilation of, *4, 15, 28, 30*

Herodotos, *9, 14, 20, 23*

hoplites, **1.2**, **2.1**

imports, *2, 5, 6, 7*, **2.3**, **2.6**, **2.7**, **2.11–12**

invasion of Attica, *4, 5, 8–9*, **2.14**, **2.16**

islands, *2, 5, 6*, **2.2**, **2.14–16**

Isokrates, *6, 22, 25, 27*

language, *12–14, 16, 18*, **2.8**

law, attitudes to *6*, **1.5**, **1.8–9**

law courts, *2, 5, 6, 7, 8, 9, 28*, **1.13**, **1.16**, **1.18**, **3.6–7**

liturgies, **1.13**, **3.4**

lot, **1.2–3**

magistracies, **1.2–3**

mass and élite, *2–3, 7, 8, 12–13, 18, 20*, **1.2**, **1.4**, **1.13–14**, **2.10**, **2.14**

Messenians, *8*, **3.11**

metics, *2, 7, 27*, **1.10**, **1.12**

Miletos, *4, 8*, **3.11**

Mysteries, profanation of *4, 15, 28, 30*

nature and purpose of work, *1–4, 10–11*

navy, and democracy, *2, 5, 7, 8, 15*, **1.2**, **1.11–12**, **1.13**, **1.19–20**, **2.2–5**, **2.11**, **2.13–14**

oral style of work, *1, 3, 10–11, 16*

orphans, *8*, **3.4**

pay, *15, 21*, **1.2–3**, **1.13**

Pericles, *5, 6, 9, 10, 11, 20, 22, 23, 25, 26*

Persia, *15, 23*

Plato, *Laws 24, 25; Menexenos 3, 7, 10, 11; Phaidros 11; Protagoras 20; Republic 7*

Pylos, *4, 25*

revenue, **1.16–18**

Samos, *4*

Sicily, *8, 15, 24*, **2.7**

slaves, *2, 7, 8, 12, 30*, **1.10–12**

Solon, *13*

tax, *7*, **1.17**

Thersites, *11*

Thucydides, *4, 5–6, 7, 8, 9, 10, 13. 14, 15, 16, 20, 21, 22, 23, 24, 25, 26, 27, 29, 30*

tribute, *4, 7, 8, 12*, **1.15**, **3.2**, **3.5**

trierarchs, *7, 8*, **1.18**, **3.4**

Xenophon, *1, 9, 13–14, 24*

Printed in the United States
by Baker & Taylor Publisher Services